How to Win Any Argument, Revised Edition

How to Win Any Argument, Revised Edition

Without Raising Your Voice, Losing Your Cool, or Coming to Blows

By Robert Mayer

THE CAREER PRESS, INC.
Pompton Plains, NJ

HOW TO WIN ANY ARGUMENT, REVISED EDITION
EDITED AND TYPESET BY NICOLE DEFELICE
Original cover design by Howard Grossman
Cover updated by Jeff Piasky
Printed in the U.S.A.

To order this title, please call toll-free 1-800-CAREER-1 (NJ and Canada: 201-848-0310) to order using VISA or MasterCard, or for further information on books from Career Press.

The Career Press, Inc.
220 West Parkway, Unit 12
Pompton Plains, NJ 07444
www.careerpress.com

Library of Congress Cataloging-in-Publication Data
Mayer, Robert, 1939 July 27-
    How to win any argument : without raising your voice, losing your cool, or coming to blows / by Robert Mayer. --Rev. ed.
        p. cm.
    Includes index.
    ISBN 978-1-60163-181-7 -- ISBN 978-1-60163-645-4 (ebook) 1. Interpersonal conflict. I. Title.

BF637.I48M4 2011
153.6--dc23
                                                                        2011026914

Dedication

Dedicated with love to the memory of my parents, Anne and Franc Mayer, whose "do the right thing" social conscience continues to be an inspiration. To my beautiful wife, Beverly, for her love, affection, and gentle, caring spirit. To Melissa, Steve, Michelle, Aaron, Zachary, and Gail.

And to Frederick J. Glassman, a great friend and law partner.

Contents

Epilogue

Introduction

Because you'll want to meet the blonde guy with the tuna melt and fries

Think about your last argument with a family member, a coworker, a supplier, a customer, a boss, a contractor, or the IRS.

Were you convinced that the other side had a closed mind? Did either side put up the same tired arguments, resisting new facts and information? Did either side overgeneralize differences, saying, "You always…," "You only…," or "You never…"? Did either side make threats they really didn't want to carry out? Did either side lose their cool? Did the other side then counter by angrily raising their voice?

Arguments Are a War of Words….

Each side digging in to defend their position. Resisting change because they are committed to the status quo…*or* because in their minds there is a justification that supports their position…*or* because they are attached to what is comfortable and familiar…*or* because their good judgment is on the line.

Each side withholding information or distorting the information they choose to give. Each side saying only those things they can say well. Each side changing from being stubbornly right to being adamantly righteous. Each side relying on their gut instincts and premonitions. And why not? It's always easier to take a stand than to understand. So, too, it's easier to decide against than to decide for.

As the war of words wages on, issues become more complex. Outcomes become less predictable. Retorts become more simplistic.

Or maybe there is silence—the hardest argument of all to refute.

This book teaches you a better way to win arguments without quarreling, squabbling, tussling, wrangling, bickering, raising your voice, losing your cool, or coming to blows. Win arguments without bulldozing and browbeating the other guy. Win arguments by finessing rather than forcing, kickin' butt, or being in the other guy's face.

You'll learn how to make, manage, and move arguments without offending or embarrassing anyone, including yourself. Win arguments with confidence, grace, and ease.

The art of argument. It's mysterious and powerful. It's the art of having things go your way. And the art of getting out of your own way. It's having "the moves." But it's also having "the touch."

You'll learn the way of the ancient martial arts masters. In Japanese, *ju* means "gentle," *do* means "way." *Judo* means "gentle way." The gentle way is directing rather than confronting the other guy's energy. But what you're about to discover won't turn you into a softie.

Winning isn't about pushy pitches, dolling up your ideas with rouge and rhinestones, or having a gift of gab. The winning way is to *get a grip*, because you need to be in control of how you will be; to construct a *Consent Zone*, because you need to manage emotions, not avoid them; to *link*, because you need things to *feel right* so a person will *want* to follow your lead; to *lead* with bulletproof reasoning because what you say needs to *sound right*; and to *cinch consent*, because, in the end, you want to trigger action.

There are reasons why all of us do what we do. The reasons don't have to be good reasons; they often aren't. The reasons don't have to be the product of conscious choice; they often aren't. This is a book about being people savvy. Understanding what makes people—including ourselves—tick.

You will discover what works—and what doesn't—when you are up against a stone wall, when your ideas are being rejected, or when you are confronted with hostility and anger. You'll learn how to be an uncompromising compromiser. How to finesse people who would rather be right than reasonable and stand up to people you can't stand.

Along with the moves for outgunning and outmaneuvering the other guy, you'll learn techniques for developing life skills that will dramatically enhance your chances of professional success and personal satisfaction.

The book you are holding has been revised and updated. To be right for our times, I have to say…

Welcome to the New Normal.

It's a time and place that is neither kind nor gentle. Our New Challenges are different than our Old Challenges. Conversations are tougher. Disagreements are more frequent. Conflicts are more trying.

All too often, it's the guy who has a "do it my way" style that gets his way. The guy with the Heavy Metal Moves. Unless you have a special knack for looking the other way, stay tuned. In a new chapter, you'll learn how to use Heavy Metal Moves. You won't be dissed, dismissed, or dumped on, and you'll learn how to defend against their use by that other guy.

Folks in conflict can no longer afford to hire litigation lawyers. In a new chapter, you'll discover time- and money-saving alternatives to court litigation: mediation, arbitration, collaborative. Unlike court litigation, these alternatives are private. Confidential. And nothing can happen unless *YOU* chose for it to happen. You'll choose the process that's best for you—what to do. What not to do.

By the way, if you're interested in becoming a mediator, this chapter explains the basics I teach in workshops to lawyers and non-lawyers interested in becoming full- or part-time mediators.

Will you be doing business with folks a world away? Whether you're sitting at your office keyboard or at their negotiating table, you need a global mindset to influence outcomes: how they make decisions. How to hear what isn't being said. How to bridge differences—and who gives in. A new chapter lays out your must-know basics: cross-cultural persuasion, negotiation, and conflict resolution.

Before we get started, here are a few folks I'd like you to meet.

Meet Karen From Modesto

Because there are arguments about getting engaged

"My boyfriend and I have been going together for six years. We argue about when we're getting engaged. I'm for sooner, he's for sometime in the undefined future."

It was my first book. My first radio interview. My first on-the-air telephone-in listener. With a half million or so northern California listeners tuned in, Karen had jump-started my book tour.

The show quickly took Karen off the air, saying it was unfair for her to dump her question on me rather than an advice-to-the-lovelorn columnist.

A few weeks after Karen's call, I was invited to speak at Tulane University. An MBA class said Karen's question was fair. One hour and two cups of chicory coffee later, I was speaking to a class of third-year law students. The law students disagreed with the MBA students. As a member of the Great Loophole Industry, I know that law students are programmed to disagree with everything. Sorry, law students, but I'm siding with the MBAs.

Arguing for a desired outcome is part of every relationship, including our most intimate ones. What you're about to discover isn't about making you a more effective businessperson or leader. It's about making you a more effective person, whether you're a Fortune 500 CEO or a PTA secretary. Whether you're revered or ignored. Whether your style is chess or poker. A person soliciting donations or soliciting votes. A staffer who has been given the task of crafting a knock-'em-dead proposal. A speaker striving for assent or a manager arguing for consent. Or Karen, a woman from Modesto, arguing that it's about time to make it permanent.

Meet Ken

Because he says I'm teaching you to be manipulative

Professional con artists and top-gun lawyers. Superstars selling Beverly Hills mansions, and a fire-and-brimstone evangelist selling God. Political speech writers, professional fundraisers, and psychology gurus. I met with and collected tips, tricks, and tactics from good guys and bad guys having but one thing in common: In their own respective arena, each is an impresario of influence, a master of persuasion. It is to that mix that I added my own experiences as a been-there, done-that mediator and lawyer.

"Bob, aren't you really teaching people how to be manipulative?"

Ken was a New York call-in radio show listener who didn't mince words.

Ken, please notice that the title of this book isn't *How to Stick It to Other People by Tricking Them Out of Their Money and Most Cherished Possessions*.

Al Smith, like Ken, was a New Yorker. When he was governor back in the 1920s, he was asked how he felt about prohibition and the consumption of alcohol—hot political topics of the day. His response was classic:

"If by alcohol you mean that which is the defiler of innocence, the corrupter of chastity, the scourge of disease, the ruination of the mind, and the cause of unemployment and broken families, then of course I oppose it with every resource of mind and body.

"But if by alcohol you mean that spirit of fellowship; that oil of conversation which adds lilt to the lips and music to the mouth; that liquid warmth which gladdens the soul and cheers the heart; that benefit whose tax revenue has contributed countless millions into public treasuries to educate our children, to care for the blind and treat our needy elder citizens—then with all the resources of my mind and body I favor it."

What you're about to discover is an art that can build or destroy, an art whose skillful application can be used to promote intolerance or to fight for better schools.

Meet the Blonde Guy With the Tuna Melt and Fries

Because duct tape isn't a solution

The tables at Ruby's Diner are pretty close together, so I couldn't help overhearing the conversation one table over.

The blonde guy with the tuna melt and fries was having a car problem. For the previous three days, the red warning light on his instrument panel wouldn't go out. "Well, you've got two choices. Either you get it fixed, or cover the light with a piece of duct tape," his friend suggested.

Relationships—whether brief or long-term; whether business, family, or social—are seldom glide-path smooth. Life's avenues aren't without potholes. Conflict is an inescapable part of the human condition.

The choice is yours: You can keep on driving as if conflict and glitches will somehow magically self-remedy. Or you can smoothe the course by putting into play what you'll learn on our journey that's about to begin.

So find yourself a comfortable chair. Pour yourself a cup of coffee. Sit back. Relax. By the way, don't go looking for charts, graphs, or boring stats. I've tried to make our journey entertaining as well as informative.

Let's get started.

Gain Absolute and Total Self-Control

Because winning begins by controlling how you will be

What separates the amateurs from the pros is self-mastery. How you walk the valleys. How you maneuver the turns. How you're able to get out of your own way.

Meet David

Because he knows the secrets of the Ancient Masters

"MASTERING OTHERS REQUIRES FORCE. MASTERING THE SELF NEEDS STRENGTH."
—THE *TAO TE CHING*

You won't find a single Maharishi U. sweatshirt hanging in my closet. I have never recited Zen Buddhist koans, tried to be in touch with my chi energy, or experienced the great light show.

I'm a khaki and leather laces utilitarian. A reality-based, prove-it-to-me kind of guy.

Nonetheless...

Even more impressive than David's credentials (former university professor and law school dean) was his style. How he handled himself in days of end-to-end meetings. His acute awareness and the subtle things he picked up on. How he easily overcame resistance and at the same time galvanized us all. He knew exactly what to say, and had a special sense of how and when to say it. David got others to feel what he felt, believe what he believed, think what he thought.

I later discovered that David's way was the way of the ancient Asian masters....

The ancient masters were subtle, mysterious, profound, responsive.

Watchful, like men crossing a winter stream.

Alert, like men of danger.

Courteous, like visiting guests.

What I'm about to share with you may sound like a mantra from a misty mountaintop. But if you're willing to be unconditionally receptive, you, too, will discover why David's style is so effective.

Are you ready?

Take a few slow, deep breaths.

Imagine that deep within you there's an *oasis of inner calm*. Imagine, too, a *dimension of detached awareness*. A dimension that makes it possible to see things from the vantage of a player on the field as well as an observer on the sidelines.

To imagine is to self-empower. You have just actualized what the ancient masters sought: *a still center*.

Now...

Imagine having the power to be aware of how you feel ("I feel hostile because...." "I feel angry because...").

Imagine having the power to *respond* rather than *react*. When you react, the event controls you. When you respond, you are in control. How you choose to perceive a situation will often determine its outcome.

Imagine having the power to control your anger and emotions. To be aware of your gut impulses ("What he is saying makes me want to..."). To be able to lower your voice as others are raising theirs.

Imagine having the power to be aware of the risks and consequences of giving way to your impulses ("If I give in to my impulses, then what will probably happen is...").

Imagine having the power to separate what is important from what is urgent. The power to pause. To observe. To absorb before acting. To be aware of alternative solutions and their benefits ("The best thing would be for me to...").

Nick, a Midwestern television station manager, invited me back to his office after an on-the-set interview. This plaque on Nick's wall somehow said it all:

"Every morning in Africa, a gazelle wakes up knowing it must run faster than the lion or be killed. Every morning, a lion awakens knowing it must outrun the slowest gazelle or starve to death. It doesn't matter if you are a lion or a gazelle. When the sun comes up, you'd better be running."

Nick's plaque can be summed up in three words: *business as usual.* Confrontations with people who will argue about anything. Or even worse, who will argue about nothing. Confrontations with people who argue because they would rather be right than reasonable: the bossy. The "boo leaders" who reject your ideas before you've had a chance to develop them. The bozos. The insensitive. The arrogant. The exhausting. People we dread having to talk to. People who drain our energy quarreling. People who make us feel anxious when they leave a message for us to call them back. People who cause us to be more self-critical in their presence.

If you have a job without conflict, then you don't really have a job. Each of us has aggravation, problems, frustrations. Each of our lives is made up of peaks and valleys, twists and turns. There will be days you'll play hopscotch with unicorns. Days you'll play Tokyo to your boss's Godzilla. What makes us different from each other is how we walk the valleys, how we maneuver the turns, how we carry the load. You can't always control the conflict, but, with a still center, you can always control your *reaction* to it.

In the morning, the sun will come up again. I'm not telling you that you'll be able to stop the race. But I do promise that as you discover the way to win, you'll become one hell of a runner.

Absolute and total self-control flows from a still center. Having a still center doesn't mean you'll always be in total control of conflict, but it does mean you'll always be in total control of your reaction to it.

7 Ways a Still Center Keeps You From Getting in Your Own Way

"KNOWING OTHERS IS WISDOM. KNOWING THE SELF IS ENLIGHTENMENT."
–THE *Tao Te Ching*

1. You Get in Your Own Way When You're Acting Under the Influence

Did your old gray suit (the one whose trousers have a shiny seat) suddenly become an almost new designer model when you made a lost luggage claim at the airport? Did your tax return overvalue the long-obsolete stereo and computer equipment that you donated to Goodwill? Do you skate on moral thin ice by saying, "But everyone does it"?

Your answer to these questions and others—the future of affirmative action, the rights and wrongs of abortion, gay marriage, the role of America's military and economic might, the style of shock jock Howard Stern, human cloning, the legalization of marijuana, the death penalty—is shaped by your influences.

At the FBI Academy, agents are taught that everybody is *AUI*—"acting under the influence."

Here's what I learned about being AUI from a lobster and hot dog dinner.

On the *USS Helena*, officers planned the meals for the ship's sailors. The only restriction was the mess hall budget. A group of us shavetail ensigns (Navy talk for wet-behind-the-ears, newly commissioned officers) were walking through the mess hall one evening when we heard a sailor tell a food server, "Give me a whole lot of that brown stuff." The sailor's "mystery meat" request launched what we thought was a "great plan."

Our plan was to skimp here and there. To build a budget reserve for one awesome meal. A meal that would have the crew dining instead of just chowing down. The entrée that would have the Pacific Fleet talking for weeks to come would be broiled lobster tails with sweet drawn butter. For those who didn't eat seafood, there would be a tried-and-true standby: hot dogs and beans.

The surprise was ours, the know-it-alls with the gold collar bars and the great plan. More than 90 percent of the crew opted for the hot dogs and beans!

In a volunteer Navy, many of the enlisted personnel are from small towns, farms, and parts of big cities where lobster tails aren't part of the gastronomical experience. Few knew that lobster was a pricey delicacy. And, to our disappointment, they really didn't care.

Not too long ago, I was negotiating the purchase of a palatial beachfront house for my client. It was once owned by one of Hollywood's biggest stars. The asking price was $8 million. When we were within a hundred thousand dollars or so of making a deal, the seller said, "I will accept your offer to buy if we close the sale in March, but you let me use the garden in May to entertain my East Coast relatives." The seller was AUI. He had an emotional need to show the house to his relatives who had not yet been west.

Brian, our remodeling contractor, had just installed a new sink, appliances, and lighting system in our kitchen. At the end of the day, the kitchen was filled with old copper tubing, soda cans, Styrofoam, sandwich wrappings, plastic bags, and boxes or refuse that Brian meticulously separated and deposited into three types of recycling trash containers.

Brian seemed to be a true friend of the environment. But when I walked Brian to his truck, I saw that it had Ohio license plates. Knowing he lived and worked in Los Angeles, I just had to ask why. "I keep it registered in Ohio. That way, I don't have to comply with California's strict air quality emissions requirements. None of those damn smog checks for me," he said. Brian, too, was AUI.

Redbook was AUI. It was concerned how its subscribers would react to a cover featuring Pierce Brosnan and his then-girlfriend, and now-wife, as she breastfed their son. The magazine's editor knew that a cover showing a mother breastfeeding would make some readers uncomfortable. It couldn't risk alienating subscribers who might be shocked or uncomfortable. The solution: Two different *Redbook* covers were printed. The newsstand edition shows mom breastfeeding, while subscribers got a picture of the couple simply holding the baby.

You're AUI. Your influences are a part of what makes you tick. A still center empowers you to be less reactive to influences. To be more analytical. To step back and make sense of your motives and priorities—your influences.

2. You Get in Your Own Way When You See Things the Way You Want Them to Be

Renewing my driver's license was a traumatic experience. My test answers were right on target. It was the application's hair color question that I blew.

I look at myself in the mirror every morning. I have always had brown hair. But the clerk who took my application looked me over, whited-out "brown," and quickly typed in "gray."

"Hey, my hair is brown," I insisted.

The clerk fired back, "You don't have brown hair—you are mostly gray with some strands of brown here and there."

My mirror reflected what I wanted to see.

You are in one of the city's best steak houses. Everything is a la carte. The steak is served with a parsley garnish. But then that doesn't really count. You order your filet with specific instructions. You want to make sure it will be served just the way you've been looking forward to. When it comes to your table, it's on a sizzling platter. It looks perfectly prepared. There is no doubt in your mind. It'll be well worth its $35 price, plus tax and tip, a total of $45.

Or is it?

What if your server gave you a pricing option: The filet will set you back $3 for each bite you eat. It's contemplated that you'll finish the filet in 15 bites.

Will you enjoy the filet as much if you opt for the per-bite pricing option? I wouldn't. As for the fixed price option, Woody Allen said it all in the movie *Manhattan*. Woody turns to his date during a taxi ride and says, "You look so beautiful, I can hardly keep my eyes on the meter."

How you cast a proposal will determine whether the other guy is focusing on the filet or on what it's going to cost to enjoy that filet.

You see things the way you want them to be. A still center empowers you to look at yourself and things without your rose-colored Ray-Bans.

3. You Get in Your Own Way When You Color the World With Your Expectations

Expectations influence how we process information and make decisions.

The *Washington Post* conducted its own experiment. During the busy morning rush hour, Joshua Bell, one of the world's great violinists, pretended to be a street performer at Washington, D.C.'s L'Enfant Plaza Metro station. Would commuters stop and listen? If so, would they show their appreciation by dropping money in his open violin case?

That morning, 98 percent of those who walked by didn't stop. They were oblivious to the performance. Only than one half of 1 percent stayed for more than a minute. After playing for about an hour, Bell walked away with $32. Because no one expected a world-class violinist to be playing in a Metro Station, they never saw or heard one.

You color the world with your expectations. You tend to accept as credible any evidence that supports your beliefs. So, too, you give short shrift to evidence that contradicts or challenges what you believe. A still center empowers you to consider "the why"—why you believe what you believe.

4. You Get in Your Own Way When You Conclude Facts From Your Assumptions

The Beverly Hills perfume shop's sign read "COMPARE OUR PRICES TO DUTY-FREE SHOP PRICES." After looking around the store, I told the clerk that even though they thought their prices were less than duty-free, they were mistaken. "We didn't say they were less. Our sign only says compare prices," she responded.

Quick Quiz

Four paperback volumes of Sherlock Holmes mysteries are standing on a shelf in sequential order. Each volume is 2 inches thick.

A bookworm in a straight line eats his way from page one of Volume I to the last page of Volume IV. How many inches of Sherlock Holmes mysteries did the bookworm eat?

The answer in a minute….

Here's another favorite workshop question of mine. Let's see how you do.

Joe is 30 years old. He is very shy and withdrawn, with little real interest in people or the world of reality. A meek and tidy soul, he has a need for order and structure, and has a passion for detail. Is it more likely that Joe is a salesman or a librarian?

Two-thirds of the executives who were asked about Joe pegged him as a librarian. But there are 75 times as many salespeople in the United States as there are librarians. Statistically, the greater chance is that Joe is a salesman. Just because something seems probable, doesn't make it so.

Maybe you made a fatal assumption about Joe. If so, you're in good company. Look at the fatal assumptions Wal-Mart made….

Wal-Mart built U.S.-style parking lots for its shopping centers in Mexico. But most citizens there don't own cars. City bus stops were behind the seemingly endless lots, making it a tough haul for shoppers to get their purchases home.

In Latin America, Sam's Club (Wal-Mart's discount food operation) fizzled and flopped. Shoppers who lived in cramped apartments didn't buy—or have room for—its huge multipack items.

In Brazil, Wal-Mart designed stores with U.S.-size aisles. Aisles that couldn't accommodate the crush of shoppers who did the bulk of their shopping once a month on pay day.

And look at the fatal assumptions you make about Wal-Mart....

You assume there will be a discount for large purchases you make at Wal-Mart. Value in value-sizes. At a Wal-Mart in Mesa, Arizona, a savvy reporter discovered that the 64-ounce Heinz ketchup was 25 percent more per ounce than the smaller bottle. The 16-ounce Minute Maid frozen orange juice was 51 percent more per ounce than the smaller size. The family-size container of Cool Whip was more per ounce than the tub half its size. At a Chicago Wal-Mart, two single canisters of Pringles were cheaper than the "Twin Pack" Pringles. None of the items priced by the reporter were on sale or promotion.

Note: You're not ready to read past this line until you've taken the books-on-the-shelf quick quiz.

The answer to the bookworm quiz is 4 inches. How can that be? Page one of Volume I when standing on a shelf is on the *far right* of Volume I. The last page of Volume IV when standing on a shelf is on the *far left* of Volume IV. The bookworm only ate through Volumes II and III. If you were wrong, it's because you made a false assumption.

But don't feel bad. Fewer than 10 percent of workshop students correctly answer the bookworm quiz. This is true even when the workshop is for executives and managers!

You conclude facts from your assumptions. You quickly accept the intuitive as conclusive. The apparent as real. You make assumptions about others. About facts. About circumstances. Your reality—what you believe—is largely based on your assumptions. A still center empowers you to consider whether there is a sound basis for your assumptions.

5. You Get in Your Own Way When You're Convinced That You "Know What You Know"

Okay, all you "foodies," here's a chance to show your stuff.

Texas barbecue specials are five times more common in Atlanta than in Dallas. True or false?

You are more likely to find corned beef lunch specials in Dallas than in New York. True or false?

Deep-dish pizza specials are seven times more common in Miami restaurants than in Chicago. True or False?

Stand by for the answers....

The late Roberto Goizueta, CEO of the Coca-Cola Company, reported in a Coke Annual Report to shareholders:

"After I spoke to a group of students at my alma mater, one of them asked me a simple question: which area of the world offers the Coca-Cola Company its greatest growth potential? Without hesitation, I replied 'Southern California.' They all laughed, thinking I was trying to be funny. So to drive home the point, I shared with them one very interesting fact. The per capita consumption of bottles and cans of Coca-Cola is actually lower in southern California than it is in Hungary. The students went silent."

Casinos take advantage of you being convinced you know what you know with ads touting big slot machine payoffs: "Highest payback" and "98 percent return." What isn't disclosed that often is that only one or two machines—in a casino with as many as 1,500—are that liberal.

Foster's, a major Australian brewery, was convinced that it knew what it knew when it decided to take on China's beer market in 1993. And why not? There were 1.2 billion Chinese, and beer consumption in China in the 10 preceding years had increased tenfold. The Foster's folks figured that if they sold beer to only 2 percent of the Chinese, they'd have a new market as big as its Australian market. Five years and $70 million in losses later, Foster's pulled out of China.

So what went wrong? Because Foster's knew what it knew, it underestimated local competition in a country where it was prestigious for towns big and small to have their own brand of beer. Foster's didn't take into full account the degree to which local governments work to support home-town breweries. Nor did Foster's consider that on an everyday basis, the Chinese wouldn't pay a premium for a foreign beer.

Morrie F. is a con artist. He is in the business of selling distributorships. Here's how he dupes his customers who know what they know: Morrie will sell you an exclusive territory to sell wall-mounted garage storage racks. Your territory will have 500,000 homes with garages. The customer-installed storage units will sell for $195. Your cost is $80. Morrie points out two things that are true: There is nothing else quite like these racks on the market. And everyone can use more storage space.

Morrie tells you that it's reasonable to expect that 3 percent of the homeowners will want to buy a storage unit. Three in a 100—seems as easy as fishing in a trout pond. If you sell 15,000 units (3 percent of 500,000) and realize a profit of $115 each, you will make—hold tight to your hat—$1,725,000! Even if you spend $225,000 for advertising, that's a profit of $1.5 million. Now that's something to write home about.

Morrie's 3 percent seems pretty reasonable. His math is faultless. But Morrie's entire scenario is based upon a dubious premise—that 3 percent of the homeowners will be your customers. A premise readily accepted by customers who know what they know.

Over the years, I've seen other clients lose money on "sure things" because all a boutique project needed to break even was just three customers an hour or, in a restaurant project, only 20 diners a meal.

What you "know" is a precursor to how you will react and respond to others and their ideas.

And lest I forget, according to *Forbes*, the answers to the three quiz questions are true!

You give undue credence to what you do know, and you figure that what you don't know isn't that important. Much of what you "know" to be true is questionable, incomplete, or downright false. Yet the reality in your heads is as important—as "real" to you—as the facts on the ground.

A still center empowers you to consider whether you really know what you know.

6. You Get in Your Own Way When You're Influenced by Head-Turning Tie-Ins

My in-laws don't refer to the things they bought on vacation—a cup and saucer, a carving, a wall hanging—as souvenirs or mementos. Instead they refer to these objects as "memories."

I think Fran and Lou's expression makes a lot of sense.

A handcrafted brass letter opener prompts my memories of an afternoon walking the cobblestoned streets of Budapest. That shady spot in my yard brings back memories of the great times my kids had with Casey, our Wheaton Terrier, who attained the status of a family member. Violets bring back lump-in-my-throat memories of my mother's birthdays.

Many times your feelings about an idea are because of what or whom you associate with it. The *tie-in* doesn't need to be rational, consequential, or relevant. An example: A supplier takes you to a great concert.

Subconsciously you let your positive feelings about the concert tie in to how you feel about the supplier.

Here are some head-turning tie-in examples involving famous people and well-known situations. Did any of them influence how you feel about a place, person, or product?

Credibility head-turners

Golf genius Tiger Woods plugged American Express. The then-president of American Express boasted the affinity between the values of discipline, hard work, achievement, and integrity that Tiger represents and those same values that American Express represents. Needless to say, given his front-page sexual exploits, Tiger is no longer plugging American Express.

Michael Jordan has pitched Nike shoes and apparel, Wilson sporting goods, Hanes underwear, WorldCom telephone service, Oakley sunglasses, Rayovac batteries, Wheaties cereal, Gatorade, and Coca-Cola. Maybe Jordan is right that Wheaties are good for me. But how credible is nutrition advice from a guy who also said I should be drinking Coke? The tie-in response of marketing gurus: "Who else is cooler than Michael Jordan? Nobody today better embodies the American spirit."[1]

Nostalgia head-turners

A poll revealed that most San Franciscans have never tried Rice-A-Roni. Nor did San Franciscans invent the rice-pasta combination dish in a box. So why is Rice-A-Roni pitched as "the San Francisco treat"? San Francisco is one of the most popular travel destinations in the country. Its fine restaurants are legendary. Rice-A-Roni trades on the strong positive feelings we have about the "City by the Bay."

The era spanning two decades after World War II is often viewed as a golden age. Communities were familiar, secure, and comfortable. We had stable jobs and relationships. An old-fashioned America when folks weren't in a hurry. Playing on the comfort of days gone by, Tulsa, Oklahoma, advertises itself as "America the way you remember it."

Moxie. Named the official soft drink of Maine in 2005. About half of those who've tried it report that it tastes like cough syrup. But then Moxie is the kind of soft drink you either love or spit out. Since 1884, Moxie's fanatical faithful have found the bitter, root extract drink the "elixir of life."

While giants like Coke and Pepsi are battling for cola market share, Moxie and other obscure soft drinks are thriving in local markets across the country. These regional or "cult" brands—with down-home names like Big Red, Sun Drop, and Kickapoo Joy Juice— are developed in mostly rural areas. Consumers identify with cult brands because of their ability to evoke nostalgia and a sense of regional pride.

And is this taking advantage or what? According to *Forbes* magazine, restaurant specials bearing the word *mom* on the average cost 15 percent more than the non-mom specials.

"Being cool" or prestigious head-turners

Okay, it's not the healthiest choice. But at a business dinner, the choice of champions is still steak. A steak dinner is, more than ever, a special event.

The 170-year-old cognac brand Courvoisier has launched a line of men's and women's sportswear. An ad campaign featured pink boots, a red silk dress, and diamond earrings spelling the logo "CV."

Land Rover has cachet, but few can afford the pricey four-wheel drive vehicles. The solution? Land Rover shoes. Footwear with the Land Rover logo, according to the shoe licensee, brings to mind the vehicle's vivid images of adventure, king-of-the-road supremacy, and guts. That's why Nike's Air Zoom Ultraflight has an outer shell modeled after the engine deck on a Ferrari Modena. And why a Nike's Air Jordan XVIII comes with side air flaps reminiscent of a Lamborghini's air intakes. Don't hold your breath. I don't think you'll be seeing footwear that looks like a Ford Focus.

Tie-ins are head-turners that influence how we think and feel. A head-turning tie-in can be as simple as a gift from a salesperson or being treated to dinner by someone soliciting your vote at an upcoming meeting. Tie-ins don't need to make sense to impact how you feel or think. A still center empowers you to consider whether the tie-in is relevant, appropriate, or applicable.

7. You Get in Your Own Way When You're Too Stubborn to Let Go of the Peanut

Tiny monkeys live along the African coast. They're fast and live high in the treetops, so there's no way to catch one unless you know the monkey hunter's secret. Africans drill a hole in a coconut that is just big enough for a monkey to squeeze his hand inside. The coconut milk is spilled out, and a peanut coated with honey is dropped into the hole. A monkey will always reach down into the hole to grab the peanut. With his fist clenched, the monkey's hand is bigger than the hole. As long as he holds onto the peanut, he can't shake free from the coconut. Because the monkey can only think of the peanut, he won't release his grip, even when the monkey hunters come to toss a net over him.

You, too, sometimes get in your own way by being so focused on a singular objective that you don't let go of the peanut.

Legend tells of a samurai warrior whose life's quest was to avenge the brutal slaying of his beloved master at the hands of a sadistic killer. After years of searching, the samurai at long last found the killer and engaged him in a duel. When the killer realized that it was the samurai who would prevail, he leaned forward and spit in the samurai's face. The samurai suddenly stopped fighting, returned his sword to its sheath, and walked away.

The samurai's students couldn't understand. "Why did you walk away?" they asked.

"Because," he explained, "my vengeance became personal."

Empowered with a still center, the samurai was able to get out of his own way. The monkey never did.

You get in your own way when you stubbornly refuse to let go. A still center empowers you to drop the peanut.

Keep this in mind: What makes you tick also makes the other guy tick. What causes you to get in your own way also causes him to get in his own way.

Take a Lesson From a Wise King
Because there's much to be learned from a mango tree

Once upon a time in a faraway land, a wise king wanted to teach his four sons a valuable life lesson. One winter he dispatched his oldest son to see a mango grove. As winter turned to spring, his second oldest son made the journey. The third son traveled to see the trees that summer. And in the fall, it was the youngest son's turn.

Upon the youngest boy's return, the king summoned his four sons and asked each what he had seen.

"The trees looked almost bare," reported the eldest son.

"No," argued the second son. "They are leafy and green."

"The trees I saw were blooming with clusters of tiny pink flowers," the third son reported.

"No," insisted the youngest. "They are filled with orange, yellow, and red fruit."

"My sons, each of you are right, for you each saw the trees at different times," said the king.

The lesson of the mango grove is to keep in mind that the other person and you have different frames of reference, different experiences, different ways of looking at things, different values, and, in all likelihood, you will use different words to say the same thing.

When you're aware, you don't just look—you see. You don't just listen—you hear. When you "see" and "hear," you're in *complete attendance*.

Look and Listen for "Tells"

Body signals are clues as to how the other person is receiving what you're saying. Because the clues are largely subconscious, con men appropriately call them "tells."

Anti-terrorism checkpoint personnel are trained to give more credence to tells than to the spoken word. Almost all mannerisms are important. Does she choose to sit directly across from you, indicating confidence? Or does she sit at an angle, indicating she is ill at ease? Has he removed his coat, indicating that he feels comfortable with you? Are there nods of approval? Is there head-shaking disapproval? Did you say something causing her to smile in relief?

Are his arms protectively folded across his chest? Is he showing tension through compressed lips, strained laughter, blushing, giggling, staring? Is she fidgeting? Has his tone of voice become elevated and belligerent? *Visually listening* for tells is zooming in to read the other person's fine print.

Look and Listen for Hidden Word Messages

"ONLY THE FOOLISH MAN HEARS ALL THAT HE HEARS."
—AN ANCIENT PROVERB

The other person's messages can be real, true, and reliable, or they can be lures, cover-ups, and decoys. Winners see and hear more than a person's words and more than the message that person is intending to convey. Construing words literally and accepting a person's messages at face value is not effective people-reading.

The words *incidentally*, *by the way*, and *as you already know* sound casual and incidental, but they usually introduce statements a person wants to downplay or sneak by you.

Someone tells you, "You are 100 percent correct in what you are saying, but...." Does he really feel you are 100 percent right, or is he just softening you up for the bad news?

"I'll give it my best." "I will try my hardest." These statements are clues that a person is already presupposing a high probability of failure.

Statements that start "Don't be concerned, but..." or "You have nothing to worry about..." mean only one thing: There is something to worry about.

Look and Listen for Priorities

Conversations, even small talk, are never as random or disorderly as they may seem.

Quick! Make a short list of television shows. Did you list items randomly? Or did you list them in the order of your personal preferences? In all probability, you will present or specify things in an order that is consistent with your own priorities or desires.

Points that you may have thought were throwaway points of secondary importance may be primary points to someone else. Learning to look and listen for what the other person considers critical will enable you to argue more effectively.

Look and Listen for Pronoun Clues

Somehow I just can't help myself. When I agree with the position my client takes, I subconsciously use phrases such as "*we* just won't agree to...." But when I'm dutifully following a client's instructions that are not totally to my liking, then my subconscious inclination is to say, "*My client* won't agree to...."

The pronouns that the other person uses are both a forecast of the response he is expecting from you and a reflection of how committed he is to his argued-for position.

The average person talks at the rate of only 120 words per minute, but can hear and comprehend 600 words per minute. You have the capacity to listen to the speaker's words as well as to his tells, hidden word messages, priorities, and pronoun clues. The capacity to be in what the pros call complete attendance.

Chapter Summary

Others will react the way you act. Controlling an argument begins by controlling how you will be. Self-command calls for an inner strength that can only flow from a still center.

A still center empowers you to get out of your own way.

Getting out of your own way is understanding that you are AUI, that you see things the way you want them to be. You color the world with your expectations and too readily accept anything that supports your expectations.

It is understanding that you conclude facts from your assumptions. You are convinced you know what you know. Your head is turned by tie-ins that may not be rational, consequential, or relevant. Sometimes you're too stubborn to let go of the peanut. Your judgment is clouded when your argument becomes a personal war of wills.

A still center empowers you to be in complete attendance—to be truly aware and to truly hear.

Construct a Consent Zone

Because people in the zone are less resistant and more receptive to you and your ideas

The *Consent Zone* is where you'll set the tone and mood for a no-blows argument. It's a virtual finessing place where you'll be able to elicit change without eliciting defensiveness, where you'll hit the ground walking. Where you'll manage the other person's emotions, not avoid them.

In this chapter, you'll discover how to construct a Consent Zone.

Meet Ensign Mayer, Who Was the Wrong Horse for the Course

Because you want to break through

Within days of my reporting aboard for duty, the *USS Helena* set sail for Yokosuka, Japan. In anticipation of joyous nights to come, the crew posted a giant photograph of Yokosuka's Country Plus Bar in their bunkroom. The sign outside the bar read "Beers Cold, Women Ready, Whisky."

My job was to persuade the men to stay away from the "for-you-a-special-price" girls. There I was, 22 years old, newly minted ensign, a never-been-there/never-done-that Navy veteran of two weeks, lecturing about venereal disease and life in the fast lane. Any knowledge I had on the subject was limited to an 11th-grade glance-through "reading" of Henrik Ibsen's *Hedda Gabler*.

I started to deliver my talk in quasi-clinical terms—reserved, the way a nervous father might talk to his son. I'd taken classes in public speaking and knew my message had been delivered with succinctness and clarity. In college, I would've been disappointed with less than an A for what I believed was an exemplary effort. But I wasn't in class, and Krieger, a salty boatswain's mate with 20 years in the Navy, motioned me aside and strongly suggested that he do the talking.

Krieger was able to *identify* with the men, and he broke through in a way I never could: "There'll be a lot of good-time girls waiting for you in Yokosuka, but I don't want you to touch those girls even if you're wearing two rubbers. If anybody comes back scratching, I'll personally pop them in the snot locker (Navy-speak for nose)."

Sometimes Age Is the Winner's Edge...

A marketing and consulting firm cautioned Baby Boomers to be ready for the fade-out of 20th-century icons, explaining that young people's needs are different. They've shared different experiences and have a whole new cast of heroes.

Less than half of 1 percent of people under the age of 25 name the Beatles, Bob Marley, or Jimi Hendrix among their favorite performers.

Elvis is marketed as a young, rebellious innovator by the Presley estate. One rock critic didn't pull any punches when he observed that today kids care about what's cool. And what's not cool are tourist buses filled with fat old people coming to Graceland to worship Elvis.

When I was a single guy, "dating" described an intimate relationship. But then came the yuppies who stopped calling it "dating." I can understand their thinking. "Dating" does sound like something from Paleontology 101: "I am dating Bev." The yuppies replaced "dating" with "going out." People with an intimate relationship were "going out." "Going out" isn't used as a frame of reference by today's singles, and has been superceded by "seeing" someone, as in "I am seeing Bev."

It's not good marketing to have someone in a pinstripe talking to young people. That's how a MasterCard vice president explained why City Kids produced the rap video "Master Your Future" for MasterCard. The video, which is shown in high schools throughout the country, explains why maintaining a good credit history is "cool."

At Other Times, Gender Is the Winner's Edge....

For Ricky Ricardo, an "Ay yi yi yi yi" and a slap to his forehead said it all. Think "Lucy." Immediately you remember her for her celebrity hounding. Her off-key singing and constant scheming. And for her Ethel-befriending, Desi-imitating ways.

But Lucy Ricardo should also be remembered as TV's first feminist. A television historian wrote that *I Love Lucy* showed us something that we had never seen before on TV: that "women express themselves differently from men. They tend to focus on emotions; they seek consensus, not conflict; they disclose more of themselves in conversation; they emphasize the personal, not the impersonal."

Cultural challenges. Language challenges. Personality challenges. Gender challenges. Age challenges. Perception challenges. Who should run the course? Should it be you? Or someone with whom the other person can identify? Or maybe someone else altogether?

Be a Thermostat, Not a Thermometer

Because you want to set the climate to "win"

Television history is dotted with long-running series that were not critically acclaimed. These shows, however, provided viewers with a star that audiences wanted in their homes for a long time and with whom they felt "really comfortable," commented the president of CBS Entertainment.

The cosmetic area of a department store can be intimidating and overwhelming. Estée Lauder "Beauty Advisors" are taught to turn browsers into buyers by quickly constructing a Consent Zone. They are coached to start with an icebreaker instead of the usual "May I help you?": "I just love what you're wearing." "Is the weather still nice outside?"

Are you more comfortable with someone who exudes optimism and enthusiasm, and has a laid-back way, or someone who is forever fretting?

Alex was a professional hypochondriac. I was his lawyer, not his doctor, but nonetheless during 20 years or so, our every conference would be preceded by Alex reciting a litany of his aches and pains. Alex's venting left me feeling uncomfortable. When he died at age 80, a member of my staff suggested that Alex's gravestone read "See! I told you I was sick!"

We all have problems. Truth is, my problems will never seem as big to you as they do to me. Nor will they ever seem as interesting, as engrossing, or as dramatic to you as they do to me. If I spend more than a few seconds laying my problems on you, you'll find being with me an uncomfortable experience.

Comfortable people are more apt to be receptive to you and your argument, to hang in there and fully hear you out, to track and consider your suggestions and reasoning.

Words of wisdom for the terminally professional: Yes, it's important to come across as knowledgeable, professional, and serious about your work. But there's a difference between being serious about what you do and being serious about who you are. The former is appreciated. The latter is not. Take yourself lightly; be able to laugh at yourself. See the potential for humor and creativity in every situation.

Not being a know-it-all means hearing what the other fellow has to say. He may surprise you with an idea you really like.

If you've ever been to San Diego, you've seen the El Cortez Hotel. The city's one-time crown jewel is a downtown landmark. It's easily recognized because although the El Cortez is an older hotel, it has an outdoor glass elevator that is consistent with much newer architecture. Before the glass elevator, the hotel only had a single interior elevator to shuttle guests between their rooms and the lobby.

Remodeling experts said the only thing that could be done do add a second elevator was to cut holes in each floor and install one. It was a plan that would have entailed a huge expense and lost income while the hotel was closed for construction. A hotel janitor mopping floors overheard the experts talking. "Why not build the elevator on the outside of the hotel?" he asked. It had never been done before, nor had the architects and engineers even considered such an idea until then. Outdoor elevators are now very much a part of the architectural scene. But the one at the El Cortez was first!

Cool It

Because "know-it-alls" don't win arguments

"IF GOD HADN'T MADE ME SO BEAUTIFUL, I'D BE A TEACHER."
—SUPERMODEL LINDA EVANGELISTA

Tulane Law School's dean confided to me, "The trouble with young professionals, particularly newly minted lawyers and MBAs from top schools, is that they are often as smug as they are bright. They talk down to other people as if they had the seasoning that only comes from years of hands-on experience."

Take the case of a brilliant 25-year-old. He was called a "Wall Street Wizard." After he was profiled in a *New York Times* article as one of the "faces of the New York economy," he was asked to resign from the elite investment banking firm Morgan Stanley.

Describing himself in the interview as young and affluent, he listed among his personal extravagances expensive electronic equipment, a Rolex watch, and a closetful of custom-made suits. So why the sudden resignation? The whiz kid broke his employer's strict code of conduct that frowns on self-aggrandizing lifestyle interviews and personal profiles.

It's not only gray flannel firms such as Morgan Stanley that discourage blatant horn-tooting. Most people react negatively to would-be persuaders who grab opportunities to brag and boast.

You may be brilliant in your field—God's gift to law, medicine, real estate, gourmet cooking—but don't wear your brilliance on your sleeve. It won't win you arguments—only resentment as a know-it-all.

Don't accept your dog's admiration as conclusive evidence that you're wonderful. Are you as brilliant as you'd like to believe? Here's the test: Think 10 years in the future. Will you know a lot then that you don't know now thanks to 10 more years of experience and learning? If so, now pause to consider how much you have yet to learn. Did you find the test humbling?

When someone else blows your horn, the sound is twice as loud. The art of subtle self-promotion is quoting clients and customers, or associates whom they know or whose reputation they respect. It's weaving real-life stories and case studies into your argument. Instead of proclaiming "We're the fastest-growing company in our field," say something more easily digested. For example, "It's not a mere accident that we're the fastest-growing company in our field. The reason is...." It's giving credit to associates and others who've helped you achieve success.

Know when to cool it. No one is ever truly influenced by a know-it-all. Or even worse, a full-of-yourself tell-it-all. Let the other guy discover for himself why he should buy into your argument from your stories and experiential anecdotes and from the praise that others have for you.

Meet Helen Bundy

Because enthusiasm is contagious

When I was about 16, I got my first "real job"—summer stockboy and sometimes salesboy (only when all the salesmen were busy) at a small men's store.

My boss, Helen Bundy, had never owned a store, nor had she ever had a job selling. She opened her shop because of a vacancy in her family's building. Long Beach, California, was a Navy town, and somehow a men's store made good sense.

Helen had a passion for her merchandise and it showed. She would greet a customer walking toward the suits, saying "Let me show you this great-looking new suit!" Helen then invited the prospect to feel the buttery texture of the gabardine or the softness of the wool flannel. Tossing a suit over her arm, Helen would dash to the dress shirt counter. "Can you believe how great this suit looks with this shirt and tie?"

What I learned about selling I learned from Helen Bundy. I would consistently run "high book," outselling the store's old pros who would ask, "You're looking for something in a suit? Are you interested in a solid color? A stripe? A glen plaid? Something in blue? Something in brown?"

The old pros were clueless. Lackluster guys with a lackluster style who never picked up on Helen's powerful secret: Enthusiasm is something you can feel right down to your toes. It's contagious. It sells. It seduces. It excites.

Is that an ab machine collecting dust in your garage? And up there on your kitchen shelf...what is that—a Chop-o-Matic? A Dial-o-Matic? A Veg-o-Matic? A Mince-o-Matic? Did you buy it through an infomercial, use it a couple of times, and then store it away? Or worse, never use it at all?

It's no wonder. You can't miss them and they're hard to resist—those bouncy, in-your-face infomercials that extol the virtues of everything from a Mr. Megamemory course to GLH Formula Number 9 Hair Thickener. And of course there is that studio audience—those regular-looking folks who are often paid to feign enthusiasm.

My brother-in-law, Dr. Eliot Phillipson, was invited by his son's elementary school teacher to participate in a class program on "what people do." Later, Eliot wrote an article about his experience in the University of Toronto's Department of Medicine's newsletter. From Eliot's article:

> "I decided to speak about scientific research and to demonstrate how it is done. The students were extremely enthusiastic about the presentation and overflowed with questions and ideas for 'future research.' I was quite confident that, when put to a vote, most of the students would opt for a career in biomedical research. A few weeks later the teacher informed me that when the students voted on what they would like to do in the future, biomedical research was ranked second. Ranked first was the retailing of double-glazed windows! The children had been tremendously impressed by the parent who was in the business of manufacturing, distributing, and installing double-glazed windows. A cynic might argue that the 'double-glazed parent' was merely a smooth, glossy salesman. But his key to winning over the students was an infectious interest in the subject, which he shared with clarity, and enthusiasm, and relevance."

Inspired enthusiasm is contagious. If you're not enthusiastic about the merits of your argument, your lack of conviction will be both apparent and contagious.

Meet Dodi Fayed

Because showing appreciation makes the other person less resistant

As everyone knows, Diana, Princess of Wales, and the man with whom she finally found happiness, Dodi Fayed, were killed when their chauffeur-driven Mercedes hit pole 13 in a Paris underpass.

Dodi Fayed was a longtime client of mine. I found him to be a likeable guy who was always appreciative of the work I did for him. Dodi's gratitude was shown in many different ways. Sometimes it was a simple "thank you." At other times it was a smoked salmon he had specially flown in from Scotland or a gigantic food package shipped from Harrods, his family's store in London.

A few months before his death, he asked me to negotiate the purchase of a home—Julie Andrews's former Malibu beachfront compound. It was an enormous task that came to fruition just before Diana and Dodi became lovers.

Dodi needed to know that he and Di would be able to enjoy their Malibu days free from intrusive paparazzi. Extra security had been put in place, and more was being planned. There was even talk of Dodi acquiring two Rottweiler guard dogs, one of whom he would name "Bob."

Appreciation can take many forms. Dodi somehow knew that I would have been pleased to share my name with a guard dog, and I told him so just a few days before he was killed.

I once overheard a handful of our firm's younger lawyers visiting with each other. The topic: Who were their favorite clients? The ones they worry about long after they've left the office for the night? Their answer: the clients who *thanked* them for their hard work and who *praised* them for their victories, big and small.

Compliments are like potato chips. After you've eaten one, you have an urge for more. People tend to live up to the compliments they receive.

Tip: General appreciation ("Good presentation, Aaron") comes across merely as an expression of good manners. Specific appreciation ("Aaron, I was particularly impressed with the way your presentation compared…") sounds less manipulative and more believable.

Some may call it sucking up or brownnosing. Others will call it strategic ingratiation. Whatever you call it, stroking works. Like it or not, kissies are the ones who are more likely to get ahead. Everyone has the basic human desire to be liked. A key to influencing outcomes is to make the other guy really think you like him, teaches a University of Minnesota psychologist.

The truth is we have trouble not liking someone who makes a fuss over us.

3 Kissie Rules

1. If you can't sound sincere when sucking up, then don't even try.

2. Only suck up to people who are just a stone's throw up the company's organizational chart from you. Praising your immediate supervisor, when deserved, is fine. A mailroom clerk laying it on

for the CEO sounds too much like the script of the Broadway musical *How to Succeed in Business Without Really Trying*.

3. Don't agree *too much* with what your boss has to say. That's not being a kissie—that's being a yes-man.

Silent appreciation doesn't mean much. Silent recognition isn't much use to anyone. A person will more readily accept your reasoning when you show recognition and appreciation for the things he or she says and does.

Consent Zone Alert

Because there are 6 common mistakes

☐ **Zone Alert #1. Don't complain or sulk.** ("You're unfair." "You're not reasonable.") A doom-and-gloom style is discomforting. A turnoff. Remember the empowering secrets of a still center and manage the curves and glitches with grace.

☐ **Zone Alert #2. Don't look back.** People look back only to criticize. Your argument goal is an agreement, not an admission or apology. Focus your argument on how something is to be done rather than on why it wasn't done that way before. Suggesting possible solutions is an *issue-management* technique that moves the focus of an argument from having to justify your complaint to your proposed remedy.

☐ **Zone Alert #3. Don't judge other people's actions or thoughts.** Judgmental words—*wrong, stupid, bad, crazy, foolhardy*—will only make a person defensive and resistant.

☐ **Zone Alert #4. Don't ask, "What is your problem?"** This makes the other person feel inadequate or lacking. It's a rare day that someone admits he was being unreasonable.

☐ **Zone Alert #5. Don't ask, "Why can't you be reasonable?"** This question invites conflict.

☐ **Zone Alert #6. Don't maneuver someone into a corner by pointing out discrepancies, proving him to be a liar.** This is an invitation to fight. Instead, go to the pro's script: "You've said A and you've said B. They are at odds with each other. How can we resolve these inconsistencies?"

It's in the Consent Zone where you'll bring emotions under control before they reach their flash point—before positions become polarized and before ideas become crystallized from having been vigorously defended.

Finesse Hostility

Because it's just like driving your car

When driving a car, you can't go from "R" to "D" without going through "N." Here's how to shift a dialogue from "Reverse" to "Neutral" so you can "Drive" your argument home.

To avoid mouth-to-mouth combat, loop the other person into your game. Try saying:

❏ "You may be right in what you are saying." This "may be" statement is non-threatening and won't prompt any new outbursts.

❏ "You are probably right." If you are reasonably sure his statement is correct, then let him know.

❏ "If I were in your shoes, I think I would feel the same way." Use this the non-provoking response if there is no possibility that he may be right. After all, if you were his mirror image— his exact alter ego—wouldn't you *have* to feel the way he does? Don't confuse *confirming* that you understand what he has said with *agreeing* with what he has said.

You can stand up to hostility and aggression. But that's not getting through. Being impossible in return is the norm. Finessing people who are hostile is the winner's art.

Meet "The Terminator"

Because you may be stuck in "R"

Simply saying "I'm sorry" isn't enough. A credible apology will say more: "I'm sorry because what I did was stupid...or silly...or greedy...or mean." An apology with too many "ifs" or "may haves" won't do the job. A genuine apology will acknowledge the offense. Offer a believable explanation for why it occurred (not to be confused with an excuse) and a sincere expression of shame. It will be an apology "for the harm that I caused" rather than an apology "in case I may have hurt you."

A first-class apology is conclusive and unequivocal...

Allegations about Arnold Schwarzenegger's attitude toward women and the accusation by six women that he touched them in a sexual manner without their consent prompted this apology:

"So I want to say to you, yes, that I have behaved badly sometimes. Yes, it is true that I was rowdy on movie sets and I have done things that were not right which I thought then was playful. But now I recognize that I have offended people. And to those people that I have offended, I want to say to them I am deeply sorry about that and I apologize."[1]

But then "The Arnold" lost ground by telling a television interviewer, "I would say most of it is not true." The accusations were just part of trash politics.

A first-class apology should contain a statement of what will be done to correct the wrong...

We're sorry for the disruption and the inconvenience the strike has caused. Thank you for your patience and understanding.... Now it's time for us to get back to the job at hand. Delivering your packages—making good on our promises. And earning back your trust. —United Parcel Service ad following the end of a teamster's union strike

But a first-class apology can also explain why the wrong can't be made right...

It was not our intention to deprive people of their rights and to cause misery, but eventually apartheid led to just that.... Deep regret goes much further than just saying you are sorry. It says that if I could turn the clock back, and if I could do anything about it, I would have liked to have avoided it." —South African President F.W. de Klerk's 1993 apology for his national party's imposition of apartheid

A first-class apology has to be delivered by a credible spokesperson...

The Deepwater Horizon disaster caused torrents of oil to spew into the Gulf of Mexico. British Petroleum's flustered CEO aired an apology that included confessing that he "wanted his life back," a comment that negatively impacted his public persona and credibility.

A first-class apology can't minimize the problem...

It's been called "Antennagate." Apple customers complained that the antenna design on the iPhone 4 caused reception problems. Apple claimed that the problem was nothing more than an easily fixed software problem. *Consumer Reports* tests confirmed that it was a hardware defect that caused the phone to lose reception when held a certain way. Apple made the public relations mistake of minimizing the problem.

A first-class apology must be timely...

Toyota recalled more than eight million vehicles because of several problems including sticky gas pedals that caused Toyotas to quickly accelerate. The carmaker had to pay a $16.4 million fine for its failure to *quickly disclose* potential safety defects.

To drive your argument forward, you may need to fess up with a genuine apology. But do it right, or don't do it at all.

Chapter Summary

Construct a Consent Zone. With the right horse for the course, resistance is minimized and receptiveness maximized. Winners are never know-it-alls or tell-it-alls. They set a winning climate. They're enthusiastic because enthusiasm is contagious. They show appreciation for the things the other person says and does. They manage emotions by finessing hostility and making tactical apologies.

Link Inside
the Consent Zone

Because people buy into trust first, ideas second

Arguments presented logically won't move someone emotionally. It's not enough that what you say *sounds right*. It must also *feel right* to the other person. Feeling right is about how *you* are rather than how *things* are.

In this chapter you'll discover things feel right when one finds comfort and credibility in what you say and do—when there's trust that you're not just "selling a bill of goods."

Take a Cue From Barbra Streisand

Because she knows the magic of a "hi-touch"

Pop diva Barbra Streisand had been unable to sing in public for years after forgetting her lines during one anxiety-filled performance. She was now back on stage at the Anaheim Pond.

Suspended from the ceiling a few rows in front of the stage were two mega TV monitors. Only Barbra and those of us lucky enough to be seated close to the stage were able to see the screens. What were they showing?

45

The words to Barbra's songs, yes—but also cues to chit-chat and share personal anecdotes and recollections throughout the evening.

Stop and think about those concerts you best recall and really loved. I'll bet they had a human force. A heart-driven connection with the audience. A "hi-touch." A touch that wasn't available on a CD. Barbra's notes to herself were reminders to occasionally stop singing and just be Barbra, to personalize her performance by reaching out and touching her audience.

Great entertainers know that their words impact an audience's intellect. But it's their touch that captures an audience's emotions. Your touch reflects the *organic* and *spiritual force* that makes you uniquely you. Your touch is reflected in your demeanor, energy, tone of voice, rate of speech, and gestures. Good or bad, your touch reflects what you as a person are all about.

Whether you're a singer or an argument pro, more than anything else, the magic of winning flows from your touch, flows from how you are, flows from how you connect.

Meet Mr. Tell-Me-More

Because he sees the really big picture

But first think about the people you know who always seem to have things go their way. Why is that?

It's a story I tell often. Tom, an investment firm manager, was looking for a college student to work for him during summer vacation. My son Steve was looking for summer employment in finance. The match was made.

"You know, Bob," Tom told me, "Steve is coming here to learn about things like index arbitrage and option contracts. But you and I both know that learning about those things is not nearly as important as the *real* lesson that can be learned here. All of my people are bright, industrious, capable, and well-informed. Yet, somehow, a handful of them are making fortunes while others are junior executives just surviving. If Steve can understand why that is, then this will be the most valuable summer of his life."

We all know people like Tom's *survivors*—people who are talented, personable, and reasonably successful at what they attempt. We also know other people who, although neither more talented nor more personable, always seem to make things happen. They are the power people, deal doers—the *winners.*

More often than not, the big difference between the winners, the survivors, and the losers is the way they interact with other people.

As I was telling the story about Steve at a Santa Monica bookstore, a graying, middle-aged man wearing a brown tweed sport coat, muted paisley tie, and sturdy wing tips loudly whispered from the front row, "Tell me more. Tell me more. Tell me more."

Mr. Tell-Me-More, you'll soon learn more about how your style—your touch—far outweighs both your IQ and your technical proficiency. Not just in your ability to win arguments, but in everything you do. About how a more effective personal style can be had by anyone who is willing to take pause from the hurry-scurry of their day to try a more effective way.

Sounding right is a cognitive thing. A logic thing. Feeling right is a people thing. A connecting, linking-up emotional thing.

Whether your argument is to many or only one, your touch—how you link with others—will impact and influence far more than the words you write, or say…or sing.

You're Always Both—the Messenger and the Message

Because content is totality

It was such a sizzling story that Court TV wanted to televise the battle between two men I will call George and Harry.

The community knew that our client, George, was a church leader, a successful physician, and a family man who was very much adored by his wife and teenage children. What they didn't know was that George was gay and had been leading a secret double life with Harry, his male lover. After a year, George told Harry he wanted to call it quits. Harry responded by threatening to tell all. To assure Harry's silence, George unwillingly supported Harry's extravagant lifestyle. At the end of six years, George couldn't take it any longer and finally said, "Enough is enough."

Harry sued, alleging George had promised to support him forever. He argued to the jury that George's gifts to him were gifts of love—freely and willingly given.

Who was to be believed? It was touch and go, and the jury could have easily gone either way. But after six days of trial, the jury found in favor of George. Afterward, some of the jurors were asked how they came to their unanimous decision. Was it our lawyers' arguments? The credibility of our witnesses? A blunder by our opponent's legal team?

The jurors acknowledged it was a tough call. But one dynamic played a key role in their deliberation: When Harry's apartment landlord and other witnesses came forward to testify about how they perceived the relationship, George raised his hand and motioned his wife and children to leave the courtroom. That gesture of sensitivity, of caring, of cocooning his family was George's way, his style, and it gave George a special credibility that made all the difference in the world.

What I learned from a battered briefcase...

I spent three days interviewing young lawyers for our firm. Each one looked very much the part. Their personalities differed, but then you don't know what someone is really like until he's working with you.

Daniel stood out in my mind. All because of his briefcase.

Like the others, Daniel was well-groomed and well-dressed. His tan briefcase, however, was battered, scarred from years of hard service. It was at odds with his shiny shoes and freshly pressed pinstripe. Curiosity got the best of me. Throwing interview protocol to the winds, I asked about the briefcase.

Daniel's father, a lawyer, died a few years before. It was his dad's briefcase. Suddenly, that beat-up old case projected an image of sensitivity and compassion. For Daniel, it was more important to carry that special case than to concern himself with what I might have thought had I not asked. Daniel's briefcase was a clear signal of what he as a person was about.

I attended a political fundraiser. One of the speakers was J.L., a well-dressed woman wearing an expensive suit with a mink-trimmed collar. The buzz in the audience was about how the speaker could be so insensitive to the feelings of animal rights advocates.

George's courtroom gesture; a battered briefcase; a mink collar. Each was a message: content is a totality. Your argument's words are only a part of your argument. The other part of your argument's content is how you are, and how I feel about you and read you. Can you be trusted? Are you concerned about my needs? Your way, your personal style, is a part of content totality. For some, J.L.'s mink collar eclipsed the words she had to say. How would you have felt about Daniel? About George?

One day you may be asked to present your argument in a talk. Here's how to save yourself a lot of aggravation and effort. Mail a copy of your talk to each person who would come to hear you. Speeches are a pain for them, too. You'll be rescuing those folks from the hassle of fighting traffic, fighting parking, and fighting for leg room. Rescued from being pulled away from things they'd rather be doing. Certainly they'll be more relaxed and better able to concentrate if they're able to peruse your words on a laid-back Sunday morning while munching on a bagel and sipping a caffe latte.

But then, maybe it's not such a great idea to scrap your talk. There's a persuasive advantage to connecting "live and in person."

According to the results of a Roper Poll, more than half of all Americans have faith and confidence in most, if not all, of what their local television newscasters report. But it's a different story when it comes to newspaper reporters. Fewer than a third of newspaper readers have that same sense of trust. Why? Trust attaches to the faces on the screens. Not to the television station or the behind-the-scenes news crew.

You're more than a walkin', talkin' word-delivery system. It's you—living, breathing you—that your audience of one or many is interested in. When you're "live and in person," you have an opportunity to connect with your whole being. To be hi-touch. To be organic. To show what you as a person are all about. To create comfort, credibility, and trust so things feel right.

Take a Cue From a Swan

Because I am...

It's that familiar feeling of no escape. Maybe it was a neighborhood mom peddling Girl Scout cookies for her daughter, or a coworker hawking raffle tickets to raise money for school band uniforms. So what if you were dieting or suffering an acute budget crunch? It's easy to say no to a cause that's not your own. But it's almost impossible to say no to someone you *like*.

When I was in fifth grade, some of my classmates were just plain popular. They were naturals. It was as if they'd been blessed with a super-likeability chromosome. Everything seemed to revolve around these naturally charismatic kids. That's probably why we called them "wheels." Wheels knew they had a *likeable* way. It's why year after year they had the guts to run for student office—and why year after year the rest of us voted for them.

I made a terrible discovery: I knew I wasn't one of the naturals—a wheel.

Maybe you aren't a natural. Few are. Maybe you aren't the "people person" you aspire to be. Or maybe you're on the quiet side. Try too hard to be likeable, and you probably won't be.

My wife, Bev, is a through-and-through people person, genuinely friendly, naturally outgoing. She's a people magnet who has nothing to sell, who isn't networking, and who isn't trying to climb a social ladder. At a social function, she immediately plugs in by introducing herself to strangers. Me? I'll still be looking for the socket—a familiar face in the crowd.

Through the years, I've made another more heartening discovery: Much of what Bev and the naturals have going for them can be adopted and put into action by anyone who is willing to change. The hi-touch way super-likeable people connect—with some effort—can become a part of what you do. And, to a real extent, who you are.

The fact that I'm not an effortless natural doesn't mean I can't adopt Bev's hi-touch style. I'm a swan. To an observer on the scene, I glide about quite gracefully. But hidden below the surface—and unlike Bev's effortless ways—there's a whole lot of paddling going on.

Winning arguments is as much about style as it is about substance. You can develop a situational style. To forge a comfort connection in settings that call for it.

Meet Greg, My Comedy Workshop Instructor

Because making things feel right is an interactive process

Sometimes I just have to do something daring. At least daring for me. I'm too much of a coward for bungee jumping or skydiving. Enrolling in a stand-up comedy workshop not only fit the "daring" bill, it gave me a chance to discover new ways to make my own workshops even more student-friendly. Greg was our comedian instructor.

In a class Greg took, he and most of his classmates weren't African-American. Nonetheless, the class instructor arranged for his students to take lessons in—are you ready for this—African dancing!

A live band played traditional African music. Drummers deftly slapped the djembe and junjun drums. The music had an ever-changing rhythm and beat. No matter how hard Greg tried, no matter how much he counted to himself, his movements were awkward. Clumsy. In music-speak, Greg couldn't "catch the groove." Sensing Greg's frustration, the band's leader clued him in to what African dancing was all about: connecting by feeling the drums…moving with the rhythm of the drums…experiencing the drums. By internalizing the beat of the drums, Greg soon found within himself the rhythm and beat that had eluded him.

In a later lesson, Greg was invited to try his hand at drumming. Even though he dabbled in various instruments and was no stranger to drums, Greg found drumming equally frustrating. No matter how hard he tried, he couldn't fall into sync with the other three drummers, who kept changing their tempo—going faster and faster, slowing down only to speed up again… but for no apparent reason. Again, the leader clued Greg in: The band's drummers were connecting by watching and following the lead dancers.

There are two things I haven't yet shared with you:

1. The class that Greg was taking was in neuro-linguistic programming—pretty heavy stuff.

2. What Greg learned in a serious behavioral class was equally relevant in a comedy workshop.

It's equally relevant to the art of argument. The dancers were connecting with and tracking the drummers. The drummers were connecting with and tracking the dancers. Each was leading, and each was following. Each was affecting, and each was being affected.

Arguing is seeking change. Change in the way the other person thinks, or feels, or sees things. Change is a process. Sometimes fast. Sometimes slow. Always affecting. Always being affected.

Meet Nike, the Shoe People

Because things feel right when you show concern

Sal T. was a client in my early days of practice. I asked Sal for a $5,000 fee advance. "Bob," he said, "just so you'll know that you never have to worry about me paying you, here's a check for $10,000." All these many years later, no other client has ever offered twice the requested advance.

We lawyers seldom ask a prospective client for information about their ability to pay beyond the initial advance. It's not until bills mount that we suddenly concern ourselves with the client's willingness—or ability—to pay the freight.

Sal racked up thousands of dollars in legal fees. As you have probably already guessed, he never paid another dime. I later learned that Sal had gotten undeserved credit from his landlord, printer, and others. Each of us got deposits in excess of what we requested. Sal's A+ creditworthiness came from his seeming *concern*. Concern evidenced by an overly sufficient deposit.

You've already found this out for yourself: Many of today's managed care doctors are juggling patients at an assembly-line pace. The frantic cadence is being set by efficiency-minded health plan administrators. Physician/patient interpersonal skills are going the way of the doctor's house call. There is no lessening of physicians' technical expertise, but patients feel less of a sense of well-being when doctor/patient interaction is sacrificed to bottom-line profits.

Bayer Pharmaceuticals came to the rescue. The aspirin folks presented physicians workshops that featured a new model for doctor-patient connecting: Show concern by really listening to the patient's story before launching into the traditional medical Q&A. Students in the School of Medicine at UCLA are coached not to listen to their patients while standing or sitting at the foot of their beds when making their hospital rounds. Concern is shown by sitting near the patient's head.

To launch its skateboarding shoe, Nike aired award-winning TV commercials. Nike's "we're concerned about skateboarders" TV pitch: "What if we treated all athletes the way we treat skateboarders?"

In skateboard's infancy, Nike seemingly wasn't concerned about the sport or about the needs of skateboarders. Skateboarders felt that Nike was ultra-uncool—arriving on the scene just in time to cash in on skateboarding's success.

A group of skateboard manufacturers rallied in support of its customers by leading a boycott against Nike. Their Johnny-come-lately battle cry: "Where was Nike when skaters were fighting to legalize our sport?" Old animosities have been forgotten, but when it counted, Nike wasn't concerned about skateboarding. When first introduced, the Nike shoe died on the shelves.

An investigative reporter pretending to be a car buyer once reported that customers are made to feel that the sales manager is tough as nails. A task master who would guzzle gasoline before he would sell you a car for a penny less than its full price. As for the salesman, he comes across as the customer's pal. Hey, if it were up to him, he'd even give you the car if he could.

Does it sound manipulative? Maybe. But a showing of concern works like a charm.

The 75/25 Partnering Secret

Here's a powerful trust-building secret: Listen, rather than talk, for at least 75 percent of your conversation. That's it—the whole secret. The secret works wonders because you seemed concerned enough to hear the other person out. Concerned enough to want to be partners in a dialogue. Concerned enough to want to talk *with* rather than talk *at*.

Things feel right when you show concern—about the other person's feelings and thoughts; by talking less and listening more; not summarily rejecting the other person's ideas; testing those ideas to see if they can be improved upon to emerge as real possibilities.

Meet David Crosby

Because he lets others discover his human condition

Yesterday, we revered the reserved. Our heroes were stoic. Aloof. Unshakable and cool. Think John Wayne, Clint Eastwood, Humphrey Bogart. A Berkeley professor who studies the language of politics reports that 50 years ago we wanted our presidents to sound elitist. Perhaps even a bit better than us. Today, those expectations are long gone. Today's culture embraces humility and vulnerability, likeability that comes from an aura of approachability, concern, and understanding. Think Elvis, JFK Jr., Ronald Reagan, Princess Diana.

When Princess Diana died, Prince Charles was chastised for not publicly putting his arms around his sons. A British journalist spoke of Charles's "emotional illiteracy." Politicians who once sought opportunities to kiss babies are connecting in ways that show us they know how to weep and hug as well. The new art is showing just how much you care and feel.

In a presidential election debate, Ronald Reagan responded to charges that he was too out of touch and too old to be running for office. His graceful response was self-deprecation: "I will not make age an issue in this campaign. I'm not going to exploit for political purposes my opponent's youth and inexperience."

Grace is having a self-deprecating sense of humor. After being seriously wounded by would-be assassin John Hinckley, Jr. in 1981, Ronald Reagan's response to his wife was, "Honey, I forgot to duck." Shortly after that attempt on his life, President Reagan's approval ratings reached 90 percent, the highest on record.

A year later, the country was recovering from an economic recession, and Reagan's poll ratings plummeted. Reagan asked his pollster, "What do the figures look like?"

"Well, they're pretty bad, Mr. President."

"How bad are they?"

"Well, they're as low as they can get. They're about 32 percent."

Reagan's face lit up and he smiled. "Don't worry. I'll just go out there and try to get shot again."

Look who else is willing to let the world know that they too are just as human as the rest of us....

Jack Chrysler is the grandson of Walter Chrysler, founder of the car company bearing his name. Needless to say, my client, Jack, has various business interests and isn't hurting. Jack's favorite is The Hitchin' Post, his Colorado country-western restaurant where there's plenty of boot-scootin' line dancing. Few customers realize that their DJ is Jack Chrysler of the Chrysler Chryslers. For fun, Jack will do private party DJ gigs in a Hitchin' Post customer's backyard. Jack's fee for a private party generally ranges between $100 and $150.

And while we're on the subject of music....

My friend David Crosby of Crosby, Stills and Nash fame was appearing in concert in Los Angeles. After his second song, the rock legend paused to hike up his pants, which had slowly started to slip south. David sheepishly smiled and confessed to the audience that he was breaking a promise to his wife—that at this special concert he wouldn't "tug his pants up" on stage. "I'm sorry, Jan," he apologized. "But honey, I just had to." We love vulnerability. The audience laughed and showed David their affection with rousing applause.

John Mauceri, as conductor of the Hollywood Bowl Orchestra, charmed summertime audiences with stories, jokes, and tidbits about family and friends. After one concert, a woman asked John's wife, Betty, "Is your husband as charming at home as he was tonight?"

Betty replied, "I guess you've never been married!" There's a little bit of situational charisma in all of us. This self-deprecating story was shared by the maestro himself as he reached out to us, his devoted audience.

Loosen up. We're all chronically human. We all have human shortcomings. Your way is credible and comfortable when you're not shy about showing yours.

Meet the Baskin-Robbins Ice Cream Man

Because you'll be surprised to learn his favorite flavor

Bob Hudecek was the president of Baskin-Robbins for 16 years. Bob told me there was one question that he was, and still is, repeatedly asked. I'll bet it's the same question you'd ask Bob if you ever met him: "What is your favorite ice cream flavor?"

Bob always answers with a question of his own: "What's yours?" No matter what flavor you choose, Bob replies, "Mine too!" By asking a question instead of responding with his personal favorite, Bob quickly connects in a way that makes you feel glad you met him. Oh, Bob's personal favorite? To this day, whenever I ask, he smiles and says, "You know, it's the same as yours."

Recall a social gathering you recently attended. Which stranger did you find the most interesting? Was it the one who showed an interest in you, your family, your work?

Okay, you have interesting things to say. But are they interesting to you or interesting to others? Link by talking to people about the things that *they* find important. Things that interest *them*.

How to Talk to People About Anything

Super salespeople are trained to spot I'm-interested-in-what-you're-interested-in bonding clues: a shirt with a golf club logo, a cap with the name of a team, a camper rather than a sedan parked in the driveway. Expand your interests and you'll bond more easily with others. Find out what's hot—movies, books, plays. And what if you aren't knowledgeable about the things the other person is into? Asking questions is listening *and* interacting.

Mary Kay Ash believed that cosmetics could be sold at home beauty shows to small groups of women looking to improve their image. Few dreamed Mary Kay would eventually be grossing more than $200 million a year. Her success was in large part attributable to one of her hi-touch rules: "Take time to make the other person feel important."

Pretend you live in a quiet middle class neighborhood. Children play on sidewalks, family pets roam from yard to yard. Three blocks away on Elm Street is a scattering of small businesses. Theatre Corp. U.S.A. wants to build a six-screen multiplex theater on Elm Street. You feel this would be a major tragedy. To your surprise, many neighbors are ambivalent. Some even look forward to being able to walk to the movies. You will be arguing for your neighbors to unite in protest against the multiplex being built. You'll be arguing with the city and Theatre Corp. that a multiplex doesn't belong on Elm Street. We'll come back to your argument as you discover the steps of having a winning argument.

Power linking is affecting and being affected. Allowing your ideas to be tested by fair and logical examination. (What do you think of a multiplex moving into the neighborhood?) Acknowledging that you understand a critical comment, but not taking the criticism personally. Here's a great way to discipline yourself to be other-centric: Imagine you're building *question sandwiches*. Set each of your questions between two generous slices of silence.

Make things feel right by being seemingly other-centric. Comfort and credibility come from serving question sandwiches to show that the other person's answer is important to you.

Meet an Infomercial Producer

Because things feel right when feelings are shared

An infomercial producer being interviewed on *60 Minutes* shared some "behind the scenes" secrets: We look for people who can prompt from the audience feelings of empathy. People who will confess that they used to be poor and overweight. Confess that they, too, had skin and hair problems.

People with whom you can identify because you feel that they were once just as you are now.

Fans will say just about anything to get their hands on a favorite author's newest book before it hits Barnes & Noble or Amazon.com. An editor at a large publishing house told me about the frantic telephone call she got from a woman who knew the power of empathy: "My father's in the hospital dying. Could you get the book to me now so he can read it before he goes?" The editor felt compelled to FedEx the printed, but not yet distributed novel. Was the woman's story true? The editor says she never really knew.

Your argument: *I know you feel that it would be nice for our kids to be able to walk to the movies. And there's no denying that a movie theatre is a place where our kids could connect with friends on Saturday afternoons. And I know you share with me an awareness of the problems a multiplex brings with it. My hope is that you're considering the minuses as well as the pluses.*

Can you ever build a feeling of togetherness without a chatty phone call or an in-person visit?

Shared feelings. A sense of emotional kinship. Few things have greater power to forge a "feels right" bond. To win assent.

How to Get Your Husband to Shed 40 Pounds

Because things feel right when power is seemingly shared

Quick Quiz

Your husband needs to shed 40 pounds. You have gone through the I-suggest-you-lose-weight phase and the nagging-and-harping phase. Now, which of the following is the most compelling thing you can say?

A. "How are you ever going to lose 40 pounds?"

B. "You must exercise more and eat less."

C. "How can you lose 40 pounds and have fun doing it?"

The quiz answer coming up soon. But first...

Almost a million boxes of Jell-O are sold every day. We're devoted to Jell-O, especially red, the flavor we hold most dear. The ease of making Jell-O was emphasized in a Norman Rockwell ad showing a little girl unmolding Jell-O for her doll. From its very first ads in 1904, Jell-O *empowered* homemakers to turn out a can't-fail dessert: "How often some ingredient is forgotten and not rightly proportioned and the dessert spoiled? This will never occur if you use Jell-O."

Even a parking space can be empowering. Bingo! You have staked out your space. The car that's there now has its reverse lights lit—a sign that the parking space's present occupant is poised to pull out. You're at the ready. The guy in the space knows you're waiting, but he isn't moving. What gives? He's just sitting there, checking out his face in the rearview mirror, messing around with his hair, adjusting his sunglasses.

A study of parking lot behavior took place at an Atlanta-area mall. On average, it takes drivers almost twice as long to back out of a parking space knowing another car is waiting for their spot. Having control over a parking space is empowering. When the space is turned over, empowerment is relinquished.

Forbes magazine calls itself "the capitalist tool." A letter in my morning mail read: "It's my pleasure to offer you an extraordinary financial tool…." Tools by their very nature are empowering devices. What tool was the letter pitching? A Visa card.

As for the husband with a weight problem, the answer is C. With choices A and B, your spouse will feel depressed and defensive. With choice C, he is likely to come up with his own answers as to how he'll shed the weight. Choice C's question is empowering.

Create an aura of interactive power. What you say feels right when power is seemingly shared. Shared power is comfortable. Your position versus the other person's position is a struggle to have power *over* rather than power *with*.

Meet the Former "Duchess of Pork"

Because unless things feel right, who cares what you say

"Meet the real exotic dancer behind tonight's movie. The news at 11!"

Local TV news lost most of its credibility with me long ago. I'm no longer coaxed to stay up by shameless tie-ins masquerading as news, suckered by promos that promised much more than they ever delivered.

In Chapter 5 you'll discover how to make your *logic* credible so things *sound* right. But here's how to make *yourself* more credible so things *feel* right.

A while back, I was lucky enough to take travel writing classes from Jack Adler, one of the best travel writers in the business. Jack's mantra was "credibility, credibility, credibility." And Jack taught us how to be credible. "Stay away from 'Gee Whiz' reporting. Superlatives can rarely be supported," he cautioned. Avoid overstatements and absolutes such as *never*, *always*, *great*, or *best*. Absolutes have a certainty and finality that are seldom true.

The defrocked Duchess of York—fresh from a divorce, notorious for tanning topless and having her toes sucked by her financial advisor—was paid $1.7 million to be a pitchwoman for Weight Watchers. Why Fergie? Once nicknamed "The Duchess of Pork," Fergie now represents honesty, one marketing consultant told a national periodical. A sample "honesty confession" from the Duchess: "Last weekend I was quite naughty. It was sausage rolls again. Sausages wrapped in phyllo pastry, cooked with fat in the oven. Yum!"

Credibility can be easily lost...

Reader Alert: If you're a Bausch & Lomb contact lens customer, then you may want to be sitting down when you read this.

Bausch & Lomb formerly sold its contact lenses under three different names. Optima FW lenses, the most expensive, were advertised to be used for one year. Medalist, the next most expensive, were advertised to be used for up to three months. SeeQuence 2, the least expensive, were advertised to be used for up to two weeks. The price difference among the three Bausch & Lomb names was significant.

Contact lens wearers like Bausch & Lomb lenses. They expect them to be high in quality. They also expect that Bausch & Lomb will make a profit—small or large—from the sale of those lenses.

Now here's what lens wearers never expected: All three brands of lenses were absolutely identical! Only their names and prices differed. State investigators in 17 states claimed the whole scenario was a scam. Bausch & Lomb said the branding was nothing more than a clever marketing strategy and denied any wrongdoing. The lenses Bausch & Lomb makes are a fine product. But the company shattered its credibility by violating consumer expectations.

Philip Morris is a good historic example of already-lost credibility. It made claims about "light" low-tar cigarettes, improved filters, or reduced smoking risks after knowing that the company had information that confirmed smoking health risks as early as 1953, but told the public that "authorities" had "reached no agreement" on what causes lung cancer.

That there was "no proof" that smoking causes cancer and that smoking is "not injurious to health." They launched a public disinformation campaign to counter mounting scientific evidence about the strong correlation between smoking and serious illness. This campaign manipulated the mass media to suppress or make light of adverse new and scientific studies.

As pressure mounted, Philip Morris announced the creation of a "research institute" dedicated to finding the "truth." Philip Morris never intended to keep its word. The institute was permitted to conduct very little research, and those results confirming the deadly link were hidden at a secret lab in Germany.

But lost credibility can be restored...

Forget about full-page color glossies of smiling flight attendants. Forget about the stats on its newest jumbo jets. Forget about the "friendly skies" hype. A while back, United Airlines wanted its stockholders to know that its primary concern is how passengers feel about their airline. Building on a we-are-learning-from-our-past theme, a United Annual Report let it all hang out by printing actual passenger complaints and vowing to do better.

A sample gripe printed in the report: a passenger commenting on Shuttle by United wrote that it "provides treatment akin to that of Trailways, Greyhound, or the worst of the bargain-basement airlines." This was United's way of telling shareholders that United must and will do better. The shareholder gripes weren't swept under the rug, but brought out in the open. Admitting the existence of specific problems, rather than talking in generalities or ignoring them, was United's way of giving shareholders assurance that things would get better. After reading unvarnished comments like that, you'd be apt to find United's promises of improvement more believable.

Do you remember this television commercial? "You tried electric. You hated it. Years ago, the whole thing just didn't feel right. This time it will. First of all, this isn't the same Norelco your father used." Were you convinced that Norelco is now doing things differently? I was.

Nike's overseas labor practices were being publicly criticized— sweatshop conditions, meager wages. Former UN Ambassador Andrew Young was hired by Nike to look into the allegations. After visiting 12 Asian factories and interviewing hundreds of workers, Young concluded: "Nike is doing a good job...but Nike can and should do better." Nike's we're-on-the-right-track response appeared in national advertisements:

"Nike agrees. Good isn't good enough in anything we do. We can and will do better."

Create an aura of credibility. If others already have positive expectations about you, don't disappoint them the way Bausch & Lomb and Philip Morris did.

Chapter Summary

The other fellow will buy into your argument when it both feels right and sounds right. Things feel right when there is a climate of credibility, comfort, and trust.

When you argue you're seeking change. Change means movement. Movement means friction. As things begin to feel right, friction fades and a link-to-lead bond emerges.

Lead Inside
the Consent Zone
Because you don't push, you lead

Arguments are won by having control over how you will be (see Chapter 1), by creating a Consent Zone before linking (see chapters 2 and 3), by linking before leading (see Chapter 4), and by leading before making your logic argument (see Chapter 5).

In this chapter, you'll discover how to lead the other person to your desired outcome.

Meet Lisa, One of Our Staffers
Because if you can't get her interested, you're going nowhere

Lisa, a member of our law office staff, is bright and well-informed. She clearly understands the health risks of smoking. Unfortunately, she has a "belief" of her own: Life is to be enjoyed and no one lives forever. If she didn't smoke, she would be a nervous wreck. She would gain weight. Smoking is bad for you, but then so are a million other things.

Who attends pro-life rallies? The answer is pro-life advocates. Who listens to pro-choice speeches? Pro-choice advocates. Who turns out to hear Republicans? Republicans turn out to hear Republicans. Democrats do the same for their candidates. Who really reads advertisements? People who have *already bought* the truck, or diet program, or personal computer being pitched.

The task of using reason to influence Lisa and others who don't already agree with you may well be an uphill battle.

How do you get people to give fat grams a second thought? By changing what they believe so they'll *want* to become actively involved in their own healthcare. How do you get people to start recycling? Start caring about endangered species? Stop polluting? By changing what they believe so they'll *want* to be partners in saving our environment. How do you get apathetic people to care about the downside of a neighborhood multiplex? By changing what they believe will happen if it's built.

People are interested in what you have to say when you show them there's something in it for them. As the story goes, a dog lover invented a new dog food. He sold his invention to one of the country's biggest dog food companies. They created a fancy package, found a mascot, and spent millions of dollars marketing the new product. But the dog food didn't sell. The marketing plan was again analyzed, but failed to explain why the dog food sat on grocers' shelves. Finally, a member of the marketing team solved the mystery: "Maybe dogs don't like our product." Your argument can be "well-packaged" and delivered with passion, but it isn't going to "sell" unless there's something in it that the other guy likes.

People aren't influenced by what you tell them. They're influenced by what they hear. Don't confuse motion with progress. Keep it simple. Keep it relevant. And keep it interesting by showing the other person what's in it for him or her.

Meet Debra, the Matchmaker
Because people judge things by comparing

Debra, who owns a successful matchmaking service, has this advice for her staff: "If you tell a woman she'll be meeting a guy who has a 'great personality and is really a hunk,' she'll be sadly disappointed if anybody short of Brad Pitt knocks at her door. But if you say her date is 'personable and has a nice appearance,' she won't be disappointed when she meets the not-so-hunky and not-so-charming Joe Average."

During a class for Beverly Hills real estate brokers, a high-earning superstar shared the logic of her of success: "Show the overpriced fixer-upper first. Later, when I take my prospects to a fairly priced home in good condition, they'll feel like they've discovered a real bargain."

Another broker told the class that she uses the same logic in reverse: "I tell prospects, 'The place I'm going to show you needs some work, but with a little imagination and effort it may fit your needs.' I then drive them to a well-maintained home in their price range. Expecting the worst, the house comes across like the Palace of Versailles."

Model home interior decorators are also masters of this *contrast tactic*. Here's the advice a decorator gave my home-builder client: If a regular-size bed will make a model bedroom look cramped, furnish the room with a crib. If the master bedroom will look skimpy with a queen or king-sized bed, furnish it with a double bed.

A tram takes visitors on the Universal Studios Tour in Hollywood through the back lot. That's where the studio stores its facades of stores, houses, and buildings. Mike, our tram guide, pointed out that the buildings had front doors of varying heights. To make larger actresses appear petite, the scene would be shot in front of a facade with an oversize door. To make a small actor appear larger, the shoot would be in front of a facade with a shorter-than-normal door.

Quick Quiz

You are an Olympic Games contender. There's slim chance you'll win a gold medal. But the chances are pretty good that you'll go home with a silver or a bronze. Will you be happier with a silver medal or with a bronze medal?

A survey of Athens Olympians revealed that silver medalists weren't as happy with their medals as were those who won bronze. Why? Because second-place winners regretted not having garnered gold. The third-place finishers were happy to have even won a coveted medal.

Pretend you've been given the news that a wealthy cousin you never met left you and other distant relatives $10,000 each. You're thrilled and excited. The next week, you learn that the amount bequeathed to those other equally distant relatives was really $50,000. Upon learning this, will you still be as happy about being left $10,000? Probably not. Happiness comes from the comparisons we make: what we have, what we expect, what we want, and what we think we deserve.

A local charity has as its annual fund-raiser: a private screening of a soon-to-be-released movie, followed by supper. The tab for the "flick'n food" is $150. Everyone knows the movie will be in general citywide distribution within a week or so of the private screening.

Here's the reasoning behind this: Charities have limited success prying loose donations when there is no corresponding donor benefit. Friends and acquaintances who receive invitations to attend the $150 screening have some wiggle room because they can decline by checking a box: "Sorry, I can't attend, but my $50 donation is enclosed."

It's like magic. Suddenly the mail is filled with $50 donations without a corresponding tangible benefit. Why? Fifty bucks is a lot of money, but compared to shelling out $150 for a movie and a not-so-great dinner, it's the deal *du jour*.

Argument pros know to seek more than they expect to receive:

"Will you chaperon Scout Camp the third *week* of January?"

"No way!"

"Well, then, how about chaperoning the snow *weekend* in October?"

"Well, I guess so."

As the local charity and the scout leader backed down from their big requests ($150 for the screening and dinner; a whole week of camp) they made smaller requests (a $50 donation; a weekend in the snow). Those smaller requests were their concessions—concessions that are gladly grabbed up by writing a check for $50 or agreeing to a few days of judging snowman-building contests.

Think back to the last time you went car shopping. Does this sound all too familiar? It's how a Honda dealer coaches its salespeople:

Lesson 1: The customer needs entry-level, two-door wheels. Show the Accord before you show the Civic. The Accord sells for about $4,000 more than a Civic. The Civic's sticker shock is softened when the prospect hears the Accord's price.

Lesson 2: The Civic comes in three models (least expensive, medium price, and luxury). If the salesperson shows the least expensive model first, the medium-price model appears expensive. If the luxury model is shown first, by comparison the medium-price model seems suddenly affordable.

Lesson 3: Hold off pitching options (fancier wheels, sound and security systems) until the basic deal has been cast. Once the customer has agreed to shell out close to $20,000, what's another $1,500 or so?

Back in the neighborhood: "We have choices. One, we can do nothing and enjoy having movies so close to home. Two, we can consent if traffic can be controlled and security is assured. Three, we can say no to the multiplex."

Quick Quiz

You are sitting down to watch TV with a bag of M&Ms. Will you eat more M&Ms if you're holding a 2-pound bag than if you're holding a 1-pound bag?

In a University of Illinois study, the average number of M&Ms consumed by those holding the 1-pound bag was 112. For those holding a 2-pound bag, it was 156. A sweet reminder that everything is relative.

People judge things by comparing them. Want to win approval for your idea? Create choices. Make your argument's desired outcome the most attractive choice you present.

4 Ways to Add Credibility to Your Argument

Because it's not enough that you're credible. What you say has to appear credible.

1. There's Credibility in Being Precise

Here's how I coached Jake, my plumber: Make a $296.75 bid and it sounds well thought out. Deliberated. But if you bid $300, it will sound "pulled out of a hat." Cavalier. An invitation to your customer to haggle.

"Ivory soap is 99-44/100 percent pure." (Would Ivory soap's purity be just as credible if it proclaimed, "Ivory soap is very, very pure"?)

"Our 747s depart on time 95 percent of the time," boasted Japan Airlines. (Would Japan Airlines's record for being on time be as credible if it proclaimed, "Our 747s are almost always on time"?)

"Clorox Clean-Up kills 99.9 percent of household bacteria and viruses." (Would Clorox Clean-Up's germ-killing ability be as credible if it proclaimed, "Hardly any household bacteria or viruses survive when you clean with Clorox"?)

The specific is more credible than the generic.

"She is consistent" is an inference. But saying "She closes seven out of 10 sales" is a credible statement of fact.

"It was a really exciting game" is a flat, lifeless abstraction. But saying "There were three touchdowns in the last 10 minutes" gives credibility to it being an exciting game.

"He is reliable" is a judgmental conclusion that doesn't convey credibility the same way "He never missed a day's work in 12 years on the job" does.

2. There's Credibility in "Who Else Says So"

It's a luxury not having to make difficult decisions—sifting through the pros and cons, evaluating the facts, gathering new facts, analyzing and separating, battling the forces of reason. It's easier to put our decision-making processes on autopilot. To simply pick up on what others have seen fit to do. We are influenced by the power of "who else says so."

My sister and I checked out at least a dozen managed-care facilities when it became apparent that my widowed dad could no longer live safely in his own home.

It was nice to tour facilities with linen tablecloths in the dining room, fresh flowers in public areas, big-screen TVs in the recreation room, caregivers in crisp white uniforms. But the place my sister and I chose for Dad had few of these amenities.

Our facility of choice was spartan and had an antiseptic quality. During my facility tour, instead of talking about how fresh the flowers were, I was introduced to occupants who couldn't recall the name of the president of the United States or the year they were born. The facility manager proudly identified those occupants for us: the former editor of the state's largest newspaper, a former top-level exec at Bank of America, and a once-prominent UCLA professor. If this facility was the choice of their caring families, then certainly it had to be our logical choice, too.

Have you ever been asked to rate a movie at a pre-release sneak preview? Or maybe you were part of an audience that was polled after a film's release.

When Warner Brothers previewed the classic film *Goodfellas,* the screening scores weren't good. Audiences said they'd be reluctant to recommend the movie to a friend. Studio pros know that the pre- and post-release polling results will generally be similar. When *Goodfellas* was finally released, critics around the country hailed it as one of the great American films. Doing an about-face, moviegoers took a cue from the critics. The post-release polling scores skyrocketed, fueled by the power of who else says so. *Goodfellas* went on to get six Oscar nominations, and *Sight & Sound* named it the fourth best film of the last 25 years.

Credibility is in the eye of the beholder...

Movie ads tout reviewers' upbeat comments. All too quickly, I choose movies because of what "those in the know" have to say. I'm constantly relearning that a movie critic's thumbs-up or four stars isn't gospel. A case in point: the big-budget musical *Moulin Rouge*, starring Nicole Kidman. In its annual year-end wrap-up, *Time*'s critics declare the best and worst movies of the year. Critic Richard Corliss named *Moulin Rouge* his "Year's Best" #2 slot. That same year, *Time*'s Richard Schickel pegged the film as #1 "Year's Worst." What is credible depends on which critic you find credible.

And there is even credibility in the not-so-credible...

A ticker-tape parade was thrown by the city of New York for its Yankees World Series champions. The mayor's office boasted to the press that a crush of 3.5 million people had lined the mile-long parade route. The 3.5 million "statistic" became widely repeated headline news.

Weeks later, an investigative reporter set the record straight: Assuming that the people standing in line were the thinnest of the thin, the line would be 1,000 people deep. An impossible feat on the cramped streets of lower Manhattan.

Call upon the logic of what other people—real or imagined—are saying: "People who have given considerable thought to the issue are very much opposed to a 6-screen theater.... Most people are saying to vote no."

3. There's Credibility in "If I Can, You Can Too"

We are influenced when we see what people who are similar to us have accomplished. It's the logic of "if I can, you can too." Show the other guy how your idea can work for him as it has worked for you and others. The testimonial is a tried-and-true advertising technique because it works. And it also works to win arguments.

Quick Quiz

You're a TV producer planning an ab-machine infomercial. Who will best sing your product's praises: A former Mr. Universe with a washboard stomach? Or Mr. Sit-in-the-Office-All-Day who burned off 3 inches of flab with your machine?

You're selling a "Math Made Easy" course. Will your best spokesperson be the professor who developed the course? Or the high school junior who went from Ds to As in three short weeks?

Infomercial testimonials feature down-the-street kinda folks. You know, the ones who bought get-rich-fast tapes and are now excitedly holding up their "trophy check"—a memorial of having closed a no-money-down or hardly-any-money down deal. Often they are plain-wrap folks with an every-man demeanor. Their implied message is crystal clear: "If I can do it, so can you!"

Multi-level marketing companies use "opportunity meetings" to recruit new distributors into their ranks. These meetings frequently feature a "lineup of stars"—real people who have achieved incredible success selling cosmetics, nutritional products, diet aids, or whatever.

4. There's Credibility by Appearing to Be "In the Know"

"Four out of five dentists recommend...." "Tylenol is the pain reliever used most." Do you remember these ads? Our world is just too complex for each of us to know a lot about everything. We rely on others to guide and inform us, and we put stock in what experts—real or perceived—have to say. We find it easy to believe what they believe.

"Shrinks Share Personal Details" was the title of a newspaper article about what's new among mental health professionals. What's new is a twist in how they go about relating to their patients. Professionals are now confiding things about themselves to their patients. One psychologist shares his experience as a child of divorce when treating patients with similar issues because sharing "can enhance the credibility of what the therapist is saying."

Estée Lauder wants you to believe what its sales clerks have to tell you. The makeup giant, which also owns Clinique, Origins, and MAC brands, now dominates the first floor of most department stores. Using it's-okay-to-believe-me titles, Estée Lauder calls its clerks "beauty advisors" and trains them to enhance their image of expertise and authority by wearing "minimum" jewelry and "neat, classic" hairstyles. Clinique clerks are "consultants," a name that creates dermatological image. Origins has "guides," a name that conveys an image of "natural" and believability. MAC clerks are "makeup artists," a name that throws off an edgier, but still in-the-know image.

Come across as someone whose logic is to be trusted. An expert...a maven...someone who has been there, done that. Be an authority, or at least have the aura of someone in the know.

Back in the neighborhood: "I met with our city councilwoman, who told me that increased traffic and noise will be unavoidable. I also met with a real estate appraiser who said that a change in the character of our neighborhood will cause our homes to be worth less."

You don't need to be in the know to appear to be in the know. Some real-life examples:

Oprah Winfrey is an expert on many topics. Mad cow disease isn't one of them. But when a food safety activist on *The Oprah Winfrey Show* suggested that mad cow disease posed a dire threat to the health of Americans who eat beef, Oprah exclaimed, "You just stopped me cold from eating another burger!" The price of cattle and cattle futures plunged the day of Oprah's television show, and Texas cattlemen filed suit against Winfrey. "People of influence have to be careful about what they say," cautioned the owner of the Amarillo Livestock Auction. The whole debacle is now known among cattlemen as "the Oprah crash."[1] Clients will sometimes ask me to form a corporation for their new start-up businesses. I usually ask why. Is there a tax reason for being incorporated? Are the checks and balances of a corporate structure necessary? Is a corporate structure needed to shelter the principals from liability? Sometimes the only reason a client will go to the expense and effort of incorporating is because, as my client H.K.

said, "It's easier to make deals when I say I am the president of a corporation...it's a position of authority. Both my business and I take on an image of importance."

C.H. is a con man who bilked millions from clients to feed his champagne appetites for contemporary art and diamonds. "Why would you doubt him?" one of his victims asked. C.H.'s victims spoke of C.H.'s "upper-crust British accent," "impeccable clothes," "nine-carat diamond ring," and "arrogance." C.H. had all the trappings and the air of authority that victims of swindlers so often cite.

Have you ever gone out to dinner with wine aficionados? You know, the folks who talk endlessly about a wine's roundness, muskiness, tannin, bouquet, and complexity. I will admit it: Sometimes I can't really tell the difference between the twist-off cap stuff and a pricey vintage offering. So what's a guy to do when he feels outgunned when it comes to having an intimate knowledge of the grape? Take a course called "How to Be a Wine Snob." And that's exactly what I did.

My taste in wine hasn't changed. But when confronted with a "What do you think of this wine?" situation, a lot of people believe I'm in the know. It's all because of the one-size-fits-all response I learned in class: With a thoughtful look, I'll nonchalantly reply, "Hmm—it's an amusing wine, but it's certainly not distinguished."

When do you feel comfortable jaywalking? Studies reveal that three-and-a-half times as many people will follow a jaywalker in a business suit crossing the street against a "DON'T WALK" sign than will follow that same jaywalker when he's dressed in a worker's shirt and pants. If he were dispensing advice, would the well-dressed fellow be more believable to you than the guy wearing a work shirt?

And while we're talking "tie power," once a year, Ben & Jerry's ice cream stores have Customer Appreciation Day, when they give away free single cones. Instead of being presented with a single scoop like everyone else in line, I was handed a double Cherry Garcia. "Why am I getting two scoops?" I asked the teenage counterman. "Don't know...guess it's 'cause you're wearing a tie."

People are influenced by the thinking of those who appear to be in the know, by the logic of "who else says so," by the logic of "if I can, you can too," by the logic of someone who has the aura and attitude of someone in the know. And sometimes by just wearing a tie!

Meet Raj, Who Telephoned Me 15 Years Later

Because stories are a powerful way to lead

Raj telephoned to say he needed a lawyer. He introduced himself by saying that 15 years earlier he attended my UCLA workshop. When we met, Raj complimented me on my negotiating skills workshop and told me how he remembered so much of what he learned that day. Raj didn't play back my serious class remarks. Instead, he talked about the anecdotes and stories I shared with the class to get those points across.

How do you create a warmth and empathy that another person can *feel*? How do you transfer emotional energy? It's easy. Tell a story.

What could be more poignant than the dripping-with-emotion Campbell's soup TV ad where a very shy young girl and her foster mother finally bond when Mom offers the girl—you guessed it!—a bowl of Campbell's soup?

Or what could be more heart-tugging than the commercial where six children from two different families try to persuade their single parents to marry? The kids' tactic: whipping up a meal for the parents that includes Campbell's soup. The parents tell the kids—now here comes the big surprise—that in fact they just got engaged!

So why doesn't Campbell's soup just come right out and tell us Campbell's soup is "M'm! M'm! Good!"? Because people are motivated when you push their emotional buttons. As for the Campbell's soup ads: "There is an emotional connection being made that transcends being hot and delicious," says the creative chief of a national advertising agency.

Stories are among the most powerful persuasive tools ever discovered by man. Jesus used them for His teaching, and we know them as parables. They've been repeated for 2,000 years. Abraham Lincoln filled his stories with a wry humor that came from his boyhood on the American frontier.

A young Abraham Lincoln was pleading a case before a jury. The circumstantial evidence was stacked against him, even though right was on his side. Lincoln persuaded the jury to ignore the logic of the circumstantial evidence by telling this story:

A farmer back home was sitting on his front porch, when suddenly his 6-year-old son came running from the barn and said, "Father, father, the hired man is in the hayloft with big sister. The hired man is pulling down his pants and big sister is lifting up her skirt, and I fear they are going to pee on the hay."

"Now, now, son," the farmer said calmly. "You have all the facts right, but you have reached the wrong conclusion."

A story is something you visualize rather than intellectualize. A story isn't something you lay on the other person. A story is something you share. It's something by which you and other people emotionally connect. A story imparts nothing to question, reject, or refute. A person who is told a story has nothing to defend.

A story transfers feelings when it is crafted in human terms rather than lifeless abstractions. Your most compelling story will be drawn from your own experience—something you saw with your own eyes, something that you heard with your own ears.

A story has the capacity to clarify the obscure and simplify the complex. The best stories are the ones you tell in plain language.

I like telling stories about growing up in the 50's. About how we played "cowboys and Indians" and ran around the neighborhood wearing cowboy hats, chaps, and carrying cap pistols.

The last time I told the story, a friend admonished me: "You can't say you played cowboys and Indians anymore. It's politically incorrect. You now have to say 'cowboys and Native Americans'." I'm sticking with plain "cowboys and Indians." It makes for a far better story.

Here's a personal favorite about how the plain language of a comic book story was long remembered....

The freighter *Al Kuwait*, carrying a cargo of 6,000 sheep, capsized in Kuwait's harbor in 1964. Fearing their water supply would be poisoned by the decaying sheep carcasses, local residents desperately needed to raise the ship from the harbor bottom. The critical question: How could the ship be raised?

A Danish manufacturer came to the rescue with an idea he'd gotten from—of all things—a 1949 Walt Disney comic book. He recalled the story of how a sunken yacht popped to the surface when Donald Duck and his nephews—Huey, Dewey, and Louie—stuffed ping pong balls into the doomed vessel.

Kuwait's water supply was spared when the Dane injected 27 billion polystyrene balls into *Al Kuwait*'s hull and the freighter rose to the harbor surface—a triumph of engineering and a long-remembered story about the creativity of four cartoon ducks.

Your story argument should have a clearly recognizable *theme*, a self-revealing reason or truth for being told. For example, in an environmental case, a lawyer made the jury want to hear more when his story began with this theme: "This is a case about whether the government has to obey the same rules as the rest of us." In another case, a lawyer's story involving a complex banking case began with this simple, compelling theme: "They lied; they stole. We want our money back."

To change how the other person feels, lead with a story. Stories are compelling, memorable, and easily understood. Stories convey warmth, empathy, and—most importantly—your human spirit.

Meet a Toyota Dealer

Because he knows there's comfort in following the lead of others

You've seen how people find comfort and guidance in doing what others are doing. Imitating saves them time and energy by validating that what they feel or think is "right on."

We all know it's okay to hoot and holler at a ball game, but not in a movie theater. And we know it's okay to pick up French fries with our fingers, but not so okay to pick up string beans or asparagus the same way. Just as it's okay to drink beer right out of the can at a barbecue, but a glass is the way to go at a nicer restaurant.

Jerry Seinfeld asks, "What's the thing with tipping jars? Is it a tip for just turning around?" Takeout-counter employees who salt their tip cups with folding money are more likely to get generous tips because "other people" have demonstrated that leaving green (rather than a coin or two) is the correct and proper thing to do. And this whole let-me-show-you-the-way thing didn't start at Starbucks. Church ushers have known for years that worshipers contribute more when collection baskets are passed around with some money already in the basket.

Customers buying cars at Southern California's largest Toyota dealership make their way past "closing tables" strategically placed around the showroom floor. Entering the dealership, the very first thing they see are customers buying Toyotas. The right-off-the-bat message: "This is the time and the place to make a really good buy on a new car."

Meet a "Low-Baller"
Because everyone needs to save face

People need to be consistent with themselves and with their previously announced beliefs.

Have you experienced either of the following examples?

❐ Dieters who announce to friends and family their commitment to shed weight are more likely to stick to their diets.

❐ Companies whose staffers are asked to write down their personal sales goals get better results than companies that don't seek written commitments.

Sellers of aluminum siding, time-share resorts, and other high-pressure hypesters all know the trick: Customers who personally fill in sales contract blanks are less likely to kill the deal during the cooling-off period.

In 25-words-or-less "Why I love..." contests, prize seekers submit brief testimonials. These testimonials become statements of commitment. The contestant, having gone on record as liking the product, is likely to remain a customer for life.

Low-balling—deliberately throwing out a lower price than one intends to charge—is an unfair sales tactic. A car dealer's confession to an investigative reporter explains how this tactic plays out:

"We tell the customer we've discovered a mistake in the quoted price. A sales manager will then apologize for reneging rather than losing money on the deal. Low-balling works because customers usually agree to the increased price because their mind-set to buy has been cast."

Call it "getting your foot in the door"—getting that small first order. A commitment—that initial order—changes a buyer's self-perception from "prospect" to "customer." With a customer's mind-set, former prospects are glad to look at samples or try other products. Doing so is consistent with being a customer. Customers have an attitude of receptiveness. People who aren't customers have an attitude of resistance.

Quick Quiz

I know. You never win anything. But pretend for the moment that in a local restaurant's drawing, you win a $125 special Saturday night dinner for two. The dinner must be enjoyed next Saturday night—no exceptions. Later in the week, you are invited to a friend's party that same Saturday. Someone you would like to meet will be at your friend's home that evening. Will you choose to have dinner at the restaurant or go to your friend's party?

Now pretend that you prepaid $125 for that special Saturday night dinner for two. The $125 is nonrefundable and the day can't be changed. Will you choose to have dinner at the restaurant or go to your friend's party?

Most people are inclined to dine with their friends in the first situation and at the restaurant in the second. Why? Because to ignore money we've already spent is being *inconsistent* with ourselves.

Our need to be consistent with ourselves is also the need to act in ways that are consistent with what others expect of us. Retreating from an announced position means appearing to others as being inconsistent. Call it the *New Revelation Tactic* revealing new information empowers a person to gracefully back down and save face. Peter Sellers, Inspector Clouseau of Pink Panther movie fame, trips in public and falls down. "I see there's nothing of interest on the floor, so I'll take a seat." Few of us can finesse embarrassment as graciously as Clouseau. Want your argument to be warmly received? Then empower the other person to sidestep from what would otherwise be the indignity of an embarrassing situation.

Back in the neighborhood: "*I discovered something you may not be aware of about what happens when multiplex theaters are built in neighborhoods like ours...*" *or* "*Here's a surprising twist on what happens to real estate value when six-screen theaters are built....*"

Do you have an about-to-be-married niece who thinks of you as being rich? If so, here's a pretty safe guess: Your inclination will be to buy her a more expensive wedding gift than you would otherwise purchase.

So why do you tip? Is it for better service? If your answer is yes, then here's a shocking fact: The relationship between the tip you leave and the future service you'll be getting is very weak, reports the *Hospitality Research Journal*. The truth is, we tip because it's expected. We act in ways that are consistent with what we believe others expect of us. And, according to University of Houston researchers, when we don't leave the expected tip, we feel embarrassment, shame, self-consciousness, and anxiety.

Did you notice? That plug of cotton in Bayer Aspirin bottles is gone! For years, cotton was the bottle's immobilizer—it kept the tablets from joggling around and breaking up. But since the 1980s, cotton really hasn't been necessary. That's when Bayer started coating its tablets with a protective microcovering. Why did Bayer wait so long? "Tradition," said a Bayer spokeswoman. Tradition for Bayer meant being consistent. We trust Bayer aspirin because it's familiar to us, and we choose it instead of chemically equivalent yet cheaper brands.

Politicians know the importance of being consistent with the expectations of voters. To remain consistent to their campaign promises not to increase taxes, presidents have gone to great lengths to avoid the "T word." During the Reagan administration, an administration official referred to a four-cents-a-gallon increase in the federal gasoline tax as a "user fee" so as not to use the word *tax*. Trying to raise taxes without saying so, President Clinton announced that his proposed healthcare plan would be partially financed by a "wage-based premium"—in other words, a tax.

Asking the other person to retreat from her announced position is asking her to be inconsistent with herself. The New Revelation Tactic gives her a graceful way to retreat from her previously taken position.

Chapter Summary

Create interest in what you have to say; otherwise your argument won't be heard.

Call on comparison power because everything you say or suggest is relative.

It's not enough that the other guy feels you're credible. What you say has to sound credible. Things sound credible when they are precise; when you call on the power of "who else says so"; the power of "if I can, you can too"; and the power of appearing to be in the know.

Lead with a story. Stories are easily understood, memorable, and compelling.

In the Consent Zone, the other person will find comfort and guidance in following your lead.

Everyone needs to be able to comfortably backpedal from their previously heels-dug-in position. The New Revelation Tactic does just that.

Create a
Bulletproof Argument

Because winning requires
"sounds right" reasoning

It's not enough that what you have to say feels right. It must also sound right. "Feeling right" is an emotional thing. "Sounding right" is a logic thing.

In this chapter, you'll discover how to make things sound right with drop-'em-in-their-tracks, argument-winning tricks.

> "LOGIC IS IN THE EYE OF THE LOGICIAN."
> —GLORIA STEINEM

When the guys on the Wilson High quad weren't talking about girls, we were exploring the magic and mystery of logic. Can you find faulty logic in this classic story that has baffled me since ninth grade? Our math teacher, Mr. Huffman, had an explanation that still rings true: Logic is both magical and mysterious.

It was a dark and stormy night. Seeking refuge from a worsening storm, three men—strangers to each other—raced into a small hotel at the same time.

The clerk tells the three men that only one room is left. A $30 room. The men agreed to share the room. Each man handed the clerk $10.

Minutes after going to the room, there was a knock on the door. It was the bellboy who said, "The desk clerk made a terrible mistake. The room is only $25." The bellboy then placed five $1 bills on a table.

Each man picked up a dollar. The remaining $2 was given to the bellboy as a tip.

The next day, one of the men told the story to his wife, "I originally paid $10, but I got back $1. So I paid $9 and contributed one-third of the $2 tip."

"Wait a minute," she said. "Three times the $9 you each paid is $27. And the $2 tip the bellboy got makes it a total of $29. What happened to the other $1?"

Logic is both truth and fiction. Reality and illusion. Magic and mystery. What seems logical to me may not seem logical to you. Logic doesn't exist in the abstract, but in the eye of the logician.

Craft a Core Argument

Because your argument must pass the Business Card Test

Have you ever walked out of a meeting without the faintest idea of what you were supposed to do? Or why you were there in the first place?

A theme puts your argument's focus where it belongs—on the forest, not the trees. Without a theme, the individual trees distract from your core argument. Set forth your theme in the simplest language possible. Every word that doesn't advance your argument hurts it.

In an example from the *Wall Street Journal*, a man murders his uncle and claims his share of the inheritance as provided for in the will. The dead uncle's wife's theme argument: A man shouldn't profit from his misdeed. The nephew's theme argument: A court must not thwart a dead man's wishes.

If there is an obvious weakness to your theme, concede it up-front. This allows the other side to focus on the facts supporting your theme: The uncle knew his nephew's propensity for violent behavior but didn't provide for disinheriting him should he act violently with the uncle.

"Eric the Bore" was my co-chair for a charity fundraiser. I spent a week with Eric one afternoon. At least, it seemed like a week. Eric is a rambler who leaves nothing out and then repeats what he said. I quickly tuned him out. It's more comfortable to jump to conclusions than suffer "death by a thousand words."

We need to have our say in order to vent our emotions, establish human contact, and feel in touch. We need to express ourselves to gain the approval of others, to display our intellect, and to give evidence of our skill and virtue. So let me ask you this: Just what do you expect to gain by using up someone else's valuable time to satisfy your personal needs?

Most of us say too much. We don't stick to the point. We tell others much more than they need or want to know. And we use 30 percent more words than are needed to drive our point home.

TV broadcasters know that attention spans are short. We seldom have any desire to hear the whole story. Here's part of a television newscast schedule that was broadcast to a region of 3 million viewers:

- ❏ Arrests made at crack house: 18 seconds.
- ❏ Suspect surrenders in shooting and robbery of tourist: 13 seconds.
- ❏ Teacher suspended for carrying concealed weapon: 59 seconds.
- ❏ Fire in Everglades almost out: 27 seconds.
- ❏ Lifeguards rescue 50 people from strong riptides: 17 seconds.
- ❏ Robbers nabbed outside grocery store: 23 seconds.
- ❏ Flooding in Illinois: 16 seconds.

Nelson Mandela made a speech on the day he was released from a South African prison after 27 years of confinement. The historic speech that marked the end to apartheid lasted less than five minutes.

People repeat themselves to emphasize their logic. But they end up over-expressing themselves. Impact increases with one or two repetitions of an idea. After that, your thoughts will be suffocated by too many words.

Are you getting ready to ramble? Tune into what you're saying. Here are a few red flags that you are about to over-express yourself: *To be quite honest with you, Basically, Essentially, Frankly.*

But what if you can't find just the right words? Silence is better than puffy fillers, go-nowhere words, *uhhs*, and *umms*. Recall the lesson of David and the ancient masters. A still center empowers you to have the sense of self-command to make your argument, then shut up. When do you stop? When you feel you've said *almost* enough.

Back in the neighborhood: "It's a trade-off: A multiplex means more traffic and more noise. On the other hand, you won't have to drive a few miles to see a movie on Saturday night."

A few cases in point:

The New Zealand captain of the *Exciter*—a super-fast Bay of Islands tour boat—had a warning for us passengers that was concise, clear, and most convincing: "Arms make a funny squishing sound when hung outside the boat while docking."

Some Americans who applauded air strikes in Afghanistan were opposed to putting U.S. ground troops in harm's way. One military spokesperson's compelling "boots on the ground" argument: No one has ever surrendered to an airplane.

The anti-rape campaign at Ohio State University produced brochures, pamphlets, and speeches. But 200 urinal screens were printed with what could best be described as a truly grabbing message: "You hold the power to stop rape in your hand."

On a Greek island cruise, Gary, a ventriloquist, and his dummy, Homer, somehow said it all.

Homer: I heard the president's speech last night. It lasted an hour and a half.

Gary: An hour and a half?! What was his speech about?

Homer: He didn't say.

Maybe Gary and Homer's routine was inspired by President John Adams's inaugural address. It had one sentence that was 727 words long! Confusing motion for progress, Fidel Castro began his speech to the United Nations by saying, "Although it has been said of us that we speak at great length, you may rest assured we shall endeavor to be brief." He then spoke for four hours and 29 minutes.

One day someone may try to present you with the Christopher Columbus Award. My advice: Turn away and run! The award is no honor. It's given to would-be persuaders who have no idea where they're going; upon arriving, don't know where they are; and when finishing up, haven't a clue where they've been.

The Business Card Test

To avoid being a Christopher Columbus Award recipient, the next time you seek to get others to think what you think, strive instead to pass the Business Card Test:

To start, write your *core argument* (why your neighbors should oppose the multiplex), on the back of a business card. If your core argument doesn't fit, then it's vague and uncertain. Work to clarify, sharpen, and simplify it.

Here's how to craft a core argument that passes the test:

You have facts and you have an analysis. Now ask yourself: *What do I conclude from all of this?* Once you reach your conclusion, you're still a ways from being done.

The next step is to ask yourself: *What do I conclude from that conclusion?* By repeating this process several more times, you will strip away all superfluous data, leaving only your core argument.

Back in the neighborhood: "If a multiplex theatre is built, our neighborhood will surely suffer."

If your core argument passes the Business Card Test, give yourself a pat on the back. It's never easy to turn your prize ox into a bouillon cube. Being able to accurately simplify your thoughts is an intellectual achievement.

My 5 Favorite Logic Tricks

Here are five of my favorite logic tricks for crafting a bulletproof core argument.

Logician Trick #1: Craft a core argument by showing an if/then correlation.

Trace evidence of material used to make bombs was found in the wreckage of TWA Flight 800. The Paris-bound plane left New York and exploded off the coast of Long Island, killing all 230 people aboard. The conclusion reached by some experts: *If* there was bomb residue, *then* the plane was blown up. It was later determined that the telltale bomb residue was left by a U.S. military unit that had chartered the plane earlier.

Logician Trick #2: Craft a core argument by expanding the realm of the possible.

If something is possible without special effort, then it must be possible with effort: A small child easily learns Spanish when it is her native language. Certainly then, a non-Hispanic college student could easily learn Spanish. (Author's note: I am living proof of the fallacy of this logic. I faithfully attended class. I sought the help of Señora Shallenberger, a tutor, who gave soul and authenticity to my lessons by wearing a silver tiara and a black Spanish-lace shawl. Despite all this, I died an excruciating death in Spanish III.)

Logician Trick #3: Craft a core argument by redefining the issue.

If the subject is abortion, the big issue is whether the subject of the abortion is a "what" or a "who." If the subject is a "what" (something that isn't yet human), then a freedom of choice can be advocated. If you define the subject as a "who" (a human being), then abortion could be condemned as manslaughter.

Logician Trick #4: Craft a core argument by redefining elements of the issue.

Pro-choice advocates argue that you define a human as having characteristics A, B, C, and D. Because an embryo at the instant of conception has none of these characteristics, it's not yet human.

Pro-life activists argue that at the moment of conception, the embryo possesses all the genetic material necessary to be a human being.

Logician Trick #5: Craft a core argument by redefining the scope of the issue.

Pro-life advocates argue that if we kill defenseless embryos, how can any member of society expect to be treated with compassion and mercy?

Pro-choice advocates argue that if a woman is denied freedom of choice within her own body, how safe are any of our freedoms?

In both arguments, the issues are expanded. The scope of the argument is no longer simply the destiny of an embryo, but the larger issues of mercy, morality, compassion, and freedom.

Getting others to buy into your logic begins with crafting a clear, concise core argument. To uncover your core argument, force yourself to repeatedly pare away the extraneous until all that's left passes the Business Card Test.

Support Your Core Argument With 3 Portable Points
Because too little is too little, and too much is too much

You've already met Greg, my stand-up comedy workshop instructor. Greg taught us that "the use of threes is a trick passed among comics as some mystical rule. A great joke is in the punch. In the unexpected. People think in patterns of three. Break the pattern's expectation and you'll get your punch—and hopefully some laughs." A workshop example:

"These dresses come in three sizes. Small, medium, and tent." (The humor doesn't come through when it's a four-word pattern: "Small, medium, large, and tent.")

Greg is right. There's a magic about threes. "Threes" are best remembered and carry max impact.

Advertisers know we're culturally attuned to messages that contain clusters of threes:

Live, love, eat!—Wolfgang Puck Cafes

No battery. Quartz accuracy. Revolutionary.—Seiko Kinetic Watches

Trustworthy, Reliable, Effectiveness.—Ricoh Business Machines

Funk, Fashion & Fettuccine.—Hollywood's Famed Sunset Strip

Italian. Sensual. Warm.—Disaronno Amaretto

Invisible. Inaudible. Incredible.—Comanche Stealth Helicopters

Snap! Crackle! Pop!—Rice Krispies

Write down the three main points that support your core argument—reasons *why* the other person should buy into your core argument. To maximize impact, ask yourself: *What do I know? What do they know? What do they need to know?* The best points are what I call *portable points*—three points out of all the possibilities that you would like the other person to take home.

Back in the neighborhood: There are three reasons why we must say no to a multiplex.

1. *Traffic will make our streets more congested, more dangerous, and more noisy.*

2. *Property values will decrease as the character of the neighborhood becomes more commercial.*

3. *Fast-food franchises and other high-traffic businesses will find it desirable to open near the multiplex, making things even worse.*

A Pig Farmer's Heads Up

But what if you have more than three main points? It's best not to strut all your stuff at once. A case in point:

A farmer owned a pig that once saved a child from being run over by a speeding car. A pig known to have ushered a family from their burning cottage. The farmer was asked, "You have an amazing pig, but why does he have a peg leg?"

"When you have a pig this great, you don't eat him all at once!" he answered.

As students, we learned that As went to the report that had the most points. A+s went to those who could back up those points with zillions of footnotes. Your English teacher *had* to read your report. That's what she was paid to do. The people you want to influence *don't have* to tune into your argument. And if it isn't compelling, they won't.

With more than three points, the important and the unimportant soon meld into a brain-deadening blur. With less than three points, your logic may appear flimsy and lacking. But logic with three supporting points discourages rebuttal and takes on powerful clarity.

How to Make Complex Points Simple

There'll be times when your core argument will be supported by *complex points*. Here's how the pros present complex points.

Break up the complex point. This will yield a pile of parts. These parts may be called steps, phases, or sections. Immediately after presenting an individual part, explain why it's important.

The result is a powerful layered effect: presentation of a part… explanation of why that part is important…presentation of another part… explanation of how that part interfaces with the previous part and why it, too, is important…and so on.

Play Your Points by the Numbers

You've discovered that having three portable points in support of your core argument is a highly effective tool. To power up your portable points, play them out by the numbers.

You'll see what I mean when you compare these two plays:

Play 1: "There are important reasons for us to oppose the multiplex…."

Play 2: "There are three important reasons for us to oppose the multiplex…."

Play 1 is humdrum and flat. Play 2 is seductive; a listener will want to listen, to focus, to start writing what you're about to say. A reader will quicken his or her reading pace to discover what the pages ahead have in store.

There's only one difference between the two plays: It's the number 3. The actual number isn't important. I was induced to read the following articles because of their intriguing numbered themes: "5 Ways to Quickly Lose Weight"; "Professional Photographers Share Their 10 Best Tips;" "6 Deadly Phrases That Will Kill Any Deal." Could you have flipped past any of these articles without giving them a chance to strut their stuff?

Using numbers to identify your portable points ("One, traffic will be heavier. Two, property values will decrease….") gives you a firm grasp on the presentation of your ideas and makes it easier for a listener or reader to track your thinking.

Getting others to buy into your logic isn't about sandbagging them with every point you can think of. It's about creating a crystal-clear *core argument* supported by three numbered *portable points*.

Logic's 3 Biggest Traps
Because you want your logic to be bulletproof

Trap #1: Illustrations are not proof. ("Let me tell you what happened last Saturday night at the Riverdale multiplex.")

An example can be found to support any point you make. Refuting examples can be found just as readily. It's risky to dwell on any *one* example. When you don't have conclusive proof, use an *assortment* of short, simple examples to back up your conclusion.

Trap #2: Common knowledge is not evidentiary. ("Everyone knows what happens when multiplexes open in quiet neighborhoods.")

All it takes to refute the statement "Everyone knows…" is to name one person who doesn't know.

Trap #3: The general is not powerful. ("It clearly goes without saying, traffic problems come with multiplexes.")

It's the specific that empowers others to envision what you envision. To be concerned about what concerns you. *"Traffic problems come with multiplexes"* is a conclusion. It doesn't hammer home your point the same way as a specific statement: *"Studies reveal that traffic in and around a 6-screen theatre can increase 20-fold on a weekend."*

Chapter Summary

Logic is both magical and mysterious. Stop-'em-in-their-tracks logic begins with a core argument supported with three portable numbered points.

Know What to Say, When to Say It, and What Not to Say

Because every argument has slippery slopes

In this chapter you'll discover eight business-as-usual argument moves. But how they play out may not be to your liking.

Meet Libby and Sam

Because they argue with Sue about schoolwork

"Our high schooler, Sue, is bright and capable. That's the good news. The bad news is that just about everything takes a priority over homework.

"We've tried the usual approaches: 'Please, I can't take it anymore. You've got to do your homework' and 'What am I going to do with you?' What arguments can we possibly make to convince Sue to get serious about school?"

From bookstore signings and radio show call-ins, it was clear what moms and dads in cities and towns big and small were thinking. When presented with similar scenarios, here are the supposedly "cool moves" and "hot tips" suggested by call-in audiences:

❏ Liking: Be incredibly nice to Sue so she will feel obligated to reciprocate by studying more. Feeling that she is liked may make Sue feel more conciliatory.

❏ Specific payoff to be earned: "Sue, if you study more, I'll increase your allowance by half."

❏ Punishment to be imposed: "Sue, if you don't study more, I'll cut your allowance in half."

❏ Personal betterment: "Sue, if you study more, it will be your gain because you'll have bettered yourself."

❏ Loss of betterment: "Sue, not studying is your loss because you're not living up to your potential."

❏ Specific payoff in advance of compliance: "Sue, I'm raising your allowance by half, but I expect you to study much more."

❏ Specific punishment in advance of compliance: "Sue, I'm cutting your allowance in half until you start studying more."

❏ Personal satisfaction: "Sue, by studying harder you'll feel better about yourself, knowing you have given school your all."

❏ Loss of satisfaction: "Sue, if you don't study you'll go through life blaming yourself for not having given the best you have to give."

❏ Appeal to morality: "Sue, it's morally wrong not to study so you can be all you can possibly be."

❏ Appeal to popular opinion: "Sue, your family and friends will be so proud of you if you get good grades."

❏ Fear of rejection: "Sue, the family will be so disappointed if you don't get good grades."

❏ Personal request: "Sue, I want you to get into a good college. As a favor to me, I want you to study harder."

❏ Sense of indebtedness: "Sue, I am sacrificing so you don't need to work after school. You owe it to me to study harder and get good grades."

❏ Logic: "Sue, college graduates earn much more than non-graduates. With that extra income, you'll be able to have a much nicer home, car, and clothes."

❐ Appeal to self-esteem: "Sue, a smart and mature person would want to study to make the most of herself."

❐ Threat to self-esteem: "Sue, it would be irresponsible and immature of you not to take full advantage of a wonderful education."

Some of these suggestions are bribes. Some are warm and fuzzy pitches. Others are bullying, whining, wheedling, plodding, prodding, threatening, intimidating, disparaging, minimizing, or strong-arming.

Which of these plays have you used in arguments? Which ones worked well for you? Which ones did not? Which of these 17 argument plays would you choose if Sue were your daughter?

A *logic play*? You can tell Sue the reasons she should study. But people reacting emotionally don't always respond to logic. Logic is a response to the reasons that Sue actually disclosed. The real problem may lie with reasons that Sue keeps to herself rather than disclosing.

A *domination play*? ("You cannot...." "I insist that you...." "You are required to...." "My policy is....") A domination play is an invitation to a power struggle. A "because I'm the mommy, that's why" argument is only effective when both parties recognize and accept the power relationship.

"Sue, you'll lose your driving privileges unless you study four hours a day" may get immediate action, but it's counterproductive in the long run. There's a difference between winning Sue's *compliance* and winning her *commitment*. Sue's fear of losing car privileges will lead to resentment. It won't lead to a true change.

A *negotiation play*? To negotiate is to compromise. By their very nature, negotiations may lead to a result where neither Mom and Dad nor Sue is completely satisfied. Besides, negotiating an agreement that Sue will study two hours each evening may not be enough to get the job done.

An *incentive play*? Giving Sue an incentive to study "tonight" or "to study all week" won't produce long-term results. You may be able to implement a long-term incentive program, but will it result in Sue developing good study habits? If there is going to be an incentive, the choice of the incentive has to be yours, not Sue's. ("Sue, don't get the impression that because we offered to let you use our car on Saturday afternoons we owe you something for doing your homework. Whether or not we offer you a reward is our choice, not yours.")

Salespeople are coached to introduce incentives by asking questions rather than touting the benefits their product or service has to offer. ("What if you could cut your telephone long-distance rates by 35 percent?")

A *threatening play*? ("You really don't want me to...." "You're forcing me to...." "You'll be sorry if you....") I was in a room where lawyers were finger-pointing and threatening each other with all sorts of retaliation. Finally, one lawyer took a deep breath and after a few moments of silence said, "Now that we've gone through all of the 'Don't-mess-with-me-I-know-karate stuff,' let's get down to business."

There are too many "never evers" in life to begin with: never ever stand until the captain turns off the seat belt sign...never ever flirt in the workplace...never ever kiss dogs on the lips...never ever buy dented canned goods...never ever use a radar detector (the cops get seriously annoyed when they pull you over and see one)...never ever hog the remote...and so on. Nonetheless, I have to add a few more to the list:

❒ Never ever make a threat without first casting it as a *soft-touch warning*: "Sue, if you don't study, I'll have no choice but to consider cutting your allowance."

❒ Never ever make a threat you don't want to carry out. Don't threaten to kick Sue out of the house if that is the last thing you would ever want to do.

❒ Never ever use a big threat in furtherance of a small gain. Telling Sue that if her grades don't improve she "will never go out on Saturday night again" won't sound credible under any circumstances. Your threat has to be proportional to its purpose and objective.

A *catastrophe-avoidance play*? I was 30 years old when my first child, Steve, was born. No sooner had the cigars been passed out than I was confronted by an endless stream of life insurance salespeople. All of them had the same pitch: If I died, Steve might not be able to go to college. My family could be forced to move to a place where danger lurked in every corner. And my wife, Bev, would be forced to work long hours just to make ends meet.

I didn't buy into their arguments and held off buying life insurance until I was in my *late* 30s. Waiting may or may not have been the wise thing to do. But then at age 30, I couldn't envision anything other than immortality. The probability of dropping dead in my tracks was beyond my contemplation.

In my freshman philosophy class, we dealt with this thorny question: Suppose state highway patrol officers no longer issued speeding tickets. Instead, a single officer would roam the highways with strict orders to summarily execute anyone caught speeding. Would our highways be safer because of the possibility of on-the-spot execution?

It is not enough to present a risk. The other person must feel that the risk is real. The class agreed that the chance of being caught was so remote that the risk of execution was almost nonexistent. There is a difference between a possibility and a probability.

You can tell Sue that if she doesn't study she'll never be all she can be. But Sue won't be motivated unless she buys into the probability of that really happening.

A *strong-arm play*? Getting Sue to hit the books is not about strong-arming her. If Mom and Dad stop talking to Sue, cut off her allowance, don't drive her where she wants to go, or strong-arm her in other ways, she'll feel bitter. Resentful. She'll look for get-even opportunities.

An *accommodation play*? Most of us avoid confrontations because they result in anger, defensiveness, or rejection. Telling Sue "We give up. do what you want. You know how we feel, but it's your life and future." An accommodation play means giving into Sue's refusal to study. You're responding to Sue's emotions, but you're not managing them.

Chapter Summary

You have choices: what to say, when to say it, and what not to say. Some choices may work in the short-run but be detrimental in the long run. Other choices may be counterproductive from their very outset. When making a choice, keep in mind the advice of a Maine Lobsterman.

Groping along in dense coastal fog is part of being a Maine lobsterman. "How do you know where the rocks are?" newsman Walter Cronkite asked a lobsterman.

"Don't," he replied. "I know where they ain't."

And as for Libby and Sam and the choices they have, stay tuned. Chapter 11 has special strategies for finessing consent from family and friends—special strategies because long-term relationships deserve special care and handling.

Assemble an Arsenal of Magic Words and Phrases

Because the way to win is to grab, hold, and convince

Call upon words and phrases to zoom your argument from flabby and ho-hum dull to captivating and compelling.

In this chapter, you'll discover how the pros present things not as they are, but as they want them to be perceived.

It's Power-Upper Time

Because you want to "caffeinate" your argument

"You'll need a basic black dress that will always get you out of a what-to-wear jam. Jazz it up with a glittery necklace, glitzy shoes, and a gold belt, and you're off and ready for the party." It was a fashion editor's advice for young women heading off for their first year of college.

How can you power up a phrase, a sentence, or a paragraph to make it so seductive and so powerful that it reaches, grabs, holds, and convinces?

How can you power up words to slam-dunk a point?

97

How can you power up your portable points to make them more intriguing, memorable, and easily understood?

It's easy. Abandon the anemic, the rote, the stilted, and the stuffy. Power-uppers jazz up your basic plain-wrap argument.

Power-Upper #1: Craft analogies.

"THE COMPANIES THAT SUCCEED WILL BE THE ONES THAT MAKE THEIR IDEAS REAL...THAT EMPLOY GREAT METAPHORS AND ANALOGIES TO DEFINE THEIR BUSINESSES AND TELL THEIR STORIES."
—SCOTT MCNEALY, COFOUNDER OF SUN MICROSYSTEMS

Ideas become explosive when you call upon the awesome power of analogies.

Microsoft monopolized the Internet browser market by bundling its browser with its Windows operating system—a market in which it already had a monopoly. With that allegation, the Department of Justice demanded that Microsoft bundle two browsers, its own and Netscape's, or none at all. Bill Gates's powerful analogy compared the demand to "requiring Coke to ship two cans of Pepsi with every six-pack."

It's not a beautiful city and the traffic is terrible. The air is thick with humidity and mosquitoes. But Houston is a city built on a swamp. A local marketing firm launched an on-line campaign seeking ways to promote Houston without resorting to catchphrases that really didn't say much. A sampling of some that were used and then soon abandoned: "Houston Proud"; "Houston's Hot"; "Space City. A Space of Infinite Possibilities."

It was an analogy submitted by a local that captured national attention: "If Houston were a dog, she'd be a mutt with three legs, one bad eye, fleas the size of CornNuts, and buckteeth. Despite all that, she'd be the best dog you'd ever know."

Power-Upper #2: Impact with intensifiers.

Intensifiers are descriptive words that create visual images—attention-garnering snapshots that pique interest, making listeners and readers want to learn more.

O.J. Simpson's defense witnesses used a memorable phrase that damaged the prosecution. The witness, a DNA expert, called the Los Angeles Police Department's lab a "cesspool of contamination." Anyone who has ever been near a cesspool readily recalls the sensory, nose-pinching experience.

Intensifiers cause the other person to recall an experience of sight, sound, smell, taste, touch, pain, or pleasure. The television show *Law & Order* pitches that its plotlines have been "ripped from the headlines."

Convincing guys they need cleanser and moisturizer as much as women is a challenge. A men's skincare company met the challenge by coaching department store salespeople that men relate to sports and cars. So instead of using words such as *cleanser* and *moisturizer*, they should use words such as *tackle acne*.

Power-Upper #3: Tantalize with the unexpected.

Retire the lame and overworked. Trash the trite. Make what's old seem fresh.

Today you can buy "genuine" draft beer ("Miller Genuine Draft"), cars ("Genuine Chevrolet"), and underwear ("Genuine Jockey"). Even rhythm and blues artist Elgin Lumpkin has—if you'll excuse the pun—gotten into the act. To show that he's the real thing, Elgin has trademarked a new name: Ginuwine.

Where do you find words that snap and sparkle? Take a look at billboard and magazine ads. Which words grab you? Which words make you want to learn more? Which words make you smile?

Power-Upper #4: Replace dull numbers with grabbers.

Logic can be dull. Look how numbing, dry statistics can become grabbers—attention-getters that are understood, dramatic, and remembered.

Enough Cracker Jack has been sold to stretch end-to-end more than 63 times around the world.—Cracker Jack package

Tootsie Roll makes enough candy each year to stretch from the Earth to the Moon and back.—*Associated Press*

The 9.0 quake that hit Japan was powerful enough to have shifted the earth and "shoved the island nation one parking space to the east."—*Time Magazine*

When Mercedes-Benz introduced its new "super-luxury" Maybach automobile, *Car and Driver* dramatized its sky-high sticker price: For the price of our test car, you can buy 22 Toyota Corollas.[1]

Here's how *Newsweek* brought home what Bill Gates's wealth meant in everyday terms: Gates could buy each household in the United States a new 27-inch color television or put a new Honda Accord LX in the garage of each Washington State household. The *Wall Street Journal* calculated that if Gates paid the same percentage of his net worth for a movie ticket that the average Joe pays, the ticket would cost him $19 million.

The American Federation of Labor–Congress of Industrial Organizations dramatically demonstrated the difference in compensation between CEOs and ordinary working folks: If you're a hot-dog vendor at Disneyland making minimum wage, you'd have to work 17,852 years to equal Disney's Chief Executive Officer Michael Eisner's then–compensation package. An employee of Coca-Cola who earns $35,000 a year would have to work 207 years to earn as much as Roberto Goizueta, its late CEO.

Power-Upper #5: Call upon persuasion-speak words.

Here's how to take the "rocky" out of rocky road….

A new law client explained that she scouts the fashion capitals of Europe in search of women's handbags, which—with the exception of the designers' names and logos—she faithfully reproduces in China for mass distribution. My mistake was asking a question that began "When you *copy* these originals...." She cut me off in mid-sentence with a smile and a wink: "I don't think of myself as copying or knocking off someone else's designs. I merely *reinterpret* what they have done."

As an ensign on the *U.S.S. Helena*, I could either *dine* in the officers' wardroom or *eat* in the enlisted personnel's mess hall. I almost always headed to the wardroom. Sunday morning breakfast was the exception. The wardroom served the tired, trite, and true: bacon and eggs; pancakes and eggs; grits and eggs. But the mess hall served up what was a Sunday morning tradition: fried chicken and eggs, breakfast a mega-leap beyond the wardroom's Denny's-type fare.

I looked forward to my Sunday morning fried chicken and eggs. Until it happened. The big turnoff. One Sunday, I heard a food server yelling to a cook, "We need more mother and daughter." To this day, I still don't have an appetite for the combination dish of fried chicken and eggs.

Store windows were shattered. Kids and adults were grabbing stereos, athletic shoes, and anything else they could carry, cart, or haul. There was rioting in a Los Angeles neighborhood, and people who would normally never dream of stealing were stealing like crazy.

One teenager cradling a cardboard box in his arms was ambushed by an in-your-face reporter: "What are you stealing?" The thief snapped, "I'm not stealing!! I'm looting."

Steal. Loot. Just words?

Steal is a harsh-sounding word. From its tone, you know someone is up to no good. But *loot* has a softer sound. Its tone is gentle. Melodic. Suggestive of conduct more mischievous than criminal. Maybe that's why "lying" is bad but "fudging" about the truth is, well, less bad.

Dumps on the outskirts of cities are now called "landfills." The word *landfill* creates an image of *filling* the land rather than dumping things onto it.

It's tough to get federal appropriation money to protect yucky "swamps." So how do you go about saving swamps? By calling them "wetlands."

Pornography is soft-pedaled as "adult entertainment." Strippers as "exotic dancers." Wanting to appeal to conservative investors, casino operators have transformed Las Vegas from a town that "gambles" to one that "games."

"Used" can be turned into chichi. Goodwill "the thrift shop" is trying to convince us that it's now Goodwill "the fashion store." Goodwill stores are becoming a destination of choice, rather than one of need, by playing down "cheap" and playing up "vintage" by advertising worn jeans as "broken-in jeans"; shrunken T-shirts as "retro shirts"; beat-up leather jackets as "distressed leather jackets."

Comedian Dennis Miller argues that opponents of capital punishment would be less resistant if we relabeled the death penalty a "life relinquishment program."

Bankers don't tell their shareholders they made "bad loans." They just have "nonperforming assets."

A shop down the street advertises a box spring and mattress set as a "sleep system."

My friend Jim is overweight. *Obese*, if you want to be clinical. *Fat*, if you call 'em as you see 'em. But Jim calls himself neither. Instead he's a "champion in the war against anorexia." Too stubborn to go on a diet, Jim's doctor has put him on a "food program."

At a seminar, salespeople were taught that "customers are terrified of sales jargon...so say 'visit' instead of 'appointment.' 'Paperwork' instead of 'contract.' And 'autograph' instead of 'signature.'"

Hasbro insisted that its G.I. Joe is not a doll. At the time, the U.S. tariff code put higher duties on dolls than toys. Disagreeing, a Customs Court judge ruled that for customs purposes Joe was indeed a doll. But Hasbro knows that a boy usually wouldn't play with a doll. Once G.I. Joe cleared customs, he became an "action figure."

When the Miami Heat tied its own NBA record for scoring the fewest points in a game, coach Pat Riley didn't say the Heat's performance was awful. Or terrible. Or dreadful. Taking the rocky out of rocky road, Riley told the press that the Heat had suffered "skill erosion."

The oldest Baby Boomers have now turned 65. Boomers are famously demanding and rebellious. Marketing pros are warning, "Don't remind them that they've aged." ADT is now marketing its "ADT Medical Alert Systems" as "ADT Companion Services." Kohler, the bathroom fixture manufacturer, used to sell "shower grab bars". But now Kohler is using a more Boomer-palatable name: "Belay shower handrail." "Belay" is named for a rock-climbing technique.

Choosing the right words is a powerful logic tool. But get too carried away and you'll lose credibility. When a cruise missile crashed in 1986, the U.S. Air Force announced that it had "impacted with the ground prematurely."

Argument pros are wordsmiths. Don't call it as you see it. Call it as you want the other guy to see it. The words and names you choose will impact how the other person feels about swamps, summer sausage, and the project he or she is spending endless hours working on.

Power-Upper #6: Craft persuasion-speak labels.

"McVeigh was not a patriot. He was a terrorist. And the jury said he deserved to die."
—*Newsweek* on the trial of Oklahoma bombers Timothy J. McVeigh

Civilians are often killed by bombs. Sometimes the people doing the bombing are U.S. airmen flying combat missions. At other times they're militants detonating explosives on trains, in office buildings, or on city streets.

Whether it's the airman or Timothy McVeigh, someone who intentionally sets off a bomb is a bomber. That's a neutral and undeniable statement of fact. That bomber could also be something more: a guerilla, a soldier, a terrorist, or a patriot.

That something more is in the eyes of the beholder. The bomber, labeled a freedom fighter by some, will be labeled a murderer by others.

Until someone comes along with a label, the bomber is still just a bomber. If I tell you the bomber is a patriot—and you believe me—you will think and react differently than if I tell you he is a terrorist. But those who dispatched the terrorist on his mission will see him as a hero.

The label terrorist was never used in Reuters news stories about those responsible for the 9-11 tragedy. Except when it quoted others who were using the "T" label, the acclaimed news service opted instead for benign phrases such as "hard-line Afghan Islamists" and "hard-line Taliban." The reason? "Terrorist" is an emotionally loaded label. A judgmental label. Reuters provides stories to newspapers and media subscribers worldwide, and many throughout Islam saw the World Trade Center perpetrators as heroes or warriors rather than terrorists.

What was your attitude about Vietnam war protests? Did you un-thinkingly buy into what others told you—that the protesters were nothing more than "anti-American agitators"? When Washington hesitated over Kosovo or Bosnia, did you say we're refusing to lead? When our bomb-ers flew, did you say they're the leading edge of American imperialism? Did you readily accept President Reagan's label that Russia was the "Evil Empire" or President George W. Bush's label that Iraq, Iran, and North Korea are the "Axis of Evil"?

Be a label-smith. Craft labels that will prompt others to think what you think and see what you see.

Chapter Summary

Call upon words, phrases, and labels that propel your argument down-field. The six Power-Uppers grab attention. Highlight key concepts. Bring clarity to your argument. Zoom your points home, making them memo-rable and easily shared.

Craft Surgical
Strike Questions
Because the other person's answers will be your desired outcome

In this chapter you'll discover a true-to-life dialogue showing how questions asked, rather than statements made, win arguments. It's what argument pros call *slow squeezing*.

> "YOU WON'T HELP SHOOTS GROW BY PULLING THEM HIGHER."
> —CHINESE PROVERB.

Bev and I arrived in Zagreb, in the former Yugoslavia, on a Saturday night in November. In our room at the InterContinental Hotel was a brochure extolling the beauty of Plitvice Lakes—16 small lakes connected by waterfalls in a beautiful mountain setting.

A Sunday visit to Plitvice Lakes sounded wonderful. According to the concierge, Plitvice Lakes tour buses did not operate off-season, but public buses ran in each direction on the hour. The journey, which would take two and a half hours, cost $2.50—a true bargain. We were concerned about the weather, but the concierge assured us the tram that circled the lakes every 45 minutes was enclosed, and that a "visit to the lakes was an absolute must."

We arrived at the lakes at 1 p.m. only to discover that every restaurant and shop was locked until summer. The tram ran only every three hours in the off-season, and the next tram was two hours later. Suddenly it began raining. I'm not talking drizzle; I'm talking buckets. With no place to go, we raced back to the main highway to catch the 2 p.m. return bus.

There was no 2 p.m. bus. The 3 p.m. bus and the 4 p.m. bus passed us by. They were too full with villagers returning to their jobs in Zagreb after a weekend at home.

By 4:30, we were very concerned, anxious, and wet. There were no taxis, there were no buses, there were no restaurants. There was coldness, there was rain, there was darkness.

Sloshing down the highway, we came across a local man who offered to drive us back to the hotel for $85. I was too wet and cold to think about negotiating, and I gladly accepted without a whimper.

Before going up to my hotel room, I stopped at the assistant manager's desk, feeling some sense of drama as I stood before him soaking wet. Certainly he would be sympathetic to the plight of a shivering guest.

I was wrong. He was unprepared to reimburse me the $85 or offer even a hot bowl of soup. He did agree to explain the situation to Mr. Bratas, the manager, when he arrived in the morning.

Here's what Mr. Bratas said to me the next morning: "I have received a memo from the assistant manager explaining in detail what happened. We regret the inconvenience. The hotel, however, does not take any responsibility for what happened."

And here is how I responded: "Mr. Bratas, you may be right in what you are saying."

Acknowledging that Bratas *may be right* was both a defusing tactic and a modulating device, setting a tone for calm, nonpositional dialogue. It was also demonstrative of my having an open mind. Having a *still center* was critical. Criticizing or yelling would only have caused Bratas to become more defensive.

Addressing Bratas by name, I was both *personalizing* the link-up and reminding Bratas that he was an *active participant* in the problem-resolution process. I didn't want him to sit in silent judgment while I spun my tale of woe.

"Perhaps I am totally wrong in asking the InterContinental to reimburse me. The hotel brochure in my room encourages visits to Plitvice Lakes. Your concierge told us that it would be a wonderful, relaxing way to spend our Sunday. Am I wrong in believing that the hotel was recommending a visit to the lakes?"

Bratas had been invited to be both candid and objective with me. I needed Bratas to become involved, to evaluate the situation *with* me as part of a collaborative, nonadversarial effort. To accomplish an affecting-and-being-affected connection, I sincerely solicited Bratas's criticism of both my facts and my analysis of those facts. A position-oriented approach was painstakingly avoided.

Wanting Bratas to reciprocate, I was allowing my conclusions to be tested by his sense of what is fair and reasonable.

"I appreciate the time that was taken by your staff in explaining how to take the bus to the lakes and back. Their interest and desire to be helpful is not in question."

Staff personalities had been separated from the argument. By telling Bratas that his staff tried to be cooperative and helpful, I was setting a hotel pattern of conduct and hospitality that I expected him to abide by. If brought into our discussions, the concierge would not think my quarrel was with him personally.

"Hopefully you and the InterContinental will want to be fair with me. I don't want to appear greedy and I know you too want to resolve this situation in a manner that is both sensible and fair."

Fairness, not money, was my primary stated concern. Bratas would not fault such an approach. Not wanting to sound self-righteous, I didn't say, "Sure, the money is important, but even more important to me is whether I am being fairly treated."

"Perhaps I should really be discussing my feelings with the Inter-Continental's management in the United States. To whom do you recommend that I write? Do you think if my travel agent also wrote that it would help?"

This *veiled ultimatum* reminded Bratas that I was serious about this situation and that the problem would not end with our discussions. I was not "reporting" him to management, but I did want to discuss my *feelings* with management. Bratas was on notice that he would have to continue to deal with the problem.

"Mr. Bratas, I understand that your position is that you have no obligation to reimburse me the $85 I spent."

By acknowledging that I fully comprehend Bratas's position, I was *confirming* that I understood what he had said without *agreeing* with what he had said. By not having to reassert his position of non-responsibility, he would perhaps be less defensive.

The words *you* and *your* rather than *hotel* were being used. Even though personalities were purposely being kept out of the picture, it was still very much a person-to-person dilemma.

"I'm curious. What is the reason you do not want to reimburse me?"

My question generously presupposed that Bratas has a rationale for his stated position. This may or may not be true, but the approach would compel him to show his cards and produce the logic behind his stated position.

My *core argument* was that I was misled and therefore the hotel needed to reimburse me. My *three portable points* were cast as *surgical strike questions* that would cause Bratas to respond to my logic.

"Let me ask a few questions to make absolutely sure I understand the facts. Is the brochure in every room because the hotel recommends visits to Plitvice Lakes? Is it the duty of your concierge to assist guests with local touring? Should the concierge have dissuaded rather than encouraged us from going to the lakes?"

These pointed questions were designed to elicit answers that I knew already. The questions forced Bratas to rethink the fairness and logic behind his stated position. If Bratas was to change his mind, it would be because of *questions asked* rather than *statements made.*

"I think I understand what you're saying. The hotel has no responsibility to me because it has no control over whether buses are filled or Plitvice Lakes facilities are closed. If my understanding is wrong, please tell me."

Again, I had confirmed in positive, unsarcastic terms that I understood what Bratas told me. He had now been invited to tell me whether my perceptions were wrong—a reminder that I wanted our communications to be open and clear. More importantly, the logic and rationale behind Bratas's position had been identified and contained. This "logic" could now be openly dealt with by both of us.

Questions rather than *statements* were posed to Bratas causing him to respond with answers rather than defensive retorts. Questions also caused Bratas to remain an involved participant in my argument's *persuasive progression.*

"I know that you're trying to be fair with me."

Reminding Bratas that fairness is the standard of a mutually agreeable solution, I wanted him to continue to be worthy of my appreciation of what he, as a person, was trying to accomplish.

"The suggestion to visit the lakes was the hotel's suggestion, which was reinforced by your concierge. The concierge also knew it was off-season, so the regular tour buses would not be operating again until summer."

Do you think it's reasonable for me to expect that he would have known that Plitvice Lakes had become a desolate, off-season area?

"You're right that a concierge has the job to assist hotel guests with their travel plans. I agree with you that he probably didn't know that, on Sunday, returning buses would be too full to stop at the lakes for passengers. *What*, however, is the reason for the concierge not knowing the status of a hotel-recommended attraction?"

I had to deal with a behavioral truth: It's more important for people to be right rather than reasonable. I have reaffirmed that what Bratas told me earlier was "right." Bratas wasn't being cross-examined in front of a judge or jury. He alone would decide whether I would be a winner. If Bratas was going to change his mind, it would be for his own reasons, not mine. My job was to cause him to generate his own reasons for wanting to change.

Using the word *what* rather than *why* kept an important question from having an accusatory quality.

"One fair method of resolving this situation would be for the hotel to reimburse us the $85 we spent, minus the cost of two return bus trips and the cost of taxi fare from the bus station back to the hotel. Do you think that makes sense?"

A possibility had been presented for Bratas's evaluation. The proposed situation was not tendered as being mine or his. Instead, it *evolved* from our general dialogue without any claim of authorship. If it was rejected, it was not *my* proposal being refused, which would make it easier for me to try other possibilities.

The proposal was made only *after* the reasoning supporting the proposal had been communicated.

"If we are able to agree, then you can adjust my hotel bill. If we are unable to reach a satisfactory resolution to this situation, then I would like to discuss the matter further with whomever you believe to be the appropriate person in the United States."

I had reiterated that a no would not be conclusive. Although I didn't want to sound threatening, I did want Bratas to know where he stood with me. A harsh threat or clear warning, however, would only have destroyed the tone of objectivity I had created.

Wanting to make a positive answer as easy as possible for Bratas, I had suggested crediting my bill rather than writing a check or reimbursing me in cash. *Adjust* is a word associated with fairness and reason.

After Bratas consented to adjust the bill, I suggested it would be a nice goodwill gesture if my wife and I dined at the hotel that evening. Bratas agreed, and it is with fondness that I still remember the cherry strudel.

Chapter Summary

Surgical strike questions cause the other guy to see for himself why it makes sense to see or do it your way.

Cinch Consent

Because it's now time to slam-dunk your win

People act and react in highly predictable ways as they quest to satisfy their emotional needs.

In this chapter you'll discover how to awaken, trigger, and stimulate conscious and subconscious emotional needs—needs that can be satisfied by your argument's desired outcome. You will also learn how to cinch consent with your "call for action."

A Lesson From an Airport Men's Room

Because you want to create and direct energy

Call them tendencies. Predispositions. Impulses. Our preprogrammed subconscious responses to what goes on around us.

Some tendencies come naturally....

Negri's Occidental Hotel is located in Sonoma County, California. A bold sign above the urinals in its men's room reads: STAND CLOSE.

It's not nice to look. But if it's for the sake of science, it's not "looking" or "peeking." It's "observing." And nobody I observed was obeying Negri's instruction.

The tiles under the urinals at the JFK Airport Arrivals Building has a "familiar lemony tinge and rubber-soled shoes will stick to it." But at Amsterdam's Schiphol Airport, the tiles under the urinals would pass an army sergeant's eagle-eyed inspection. The difference isn't in the mopping. The difference is urinal flies. At Schiphol, each urinal has a fly in it—actually the black outline of a fly, etched into the porcelain. The fly prompts a man to aim. If a man sees a fly, he aims at it, a Schiphol executive explained. The fly etchings "reduce spillage by 80 percent." Schiphol's etched fly is calculated to prompt a desired autopilot reaction: aim.[1]

Other tendencies are the result of conditioning....

I will ask students questions. Those wanting to answer raise their hands. I have asked them, "Why did you raise your hands? Why didn't you stand or respond by saying 'I want to answer'?" Uniformly they answer, "Because I have always raised my hand."

Telling men to STAND CLOSE won't do the trick. But men will naturally take time to aim when presented with a target. Students are conditioned to raise their hands when answering a question.

"While the individual man is an insoluble puzzle, in the aggregate he becomes a mathematical certainty. You can, for example, never foretell what any one man will do, but you can say with precision what an average number will be up to. Individuals vary, but percentages remain constant," Sherlock Holmes advises us in *The Sign of Four*.

People aren't influenced in the abstract. People don't make decisions in the abstract. There are always reasons. Sometimes logical, sometimes emotional. Sometimes the product of the highly predictable subconscious, emotion-driven tendencies of which Holmes spoke.

Tendencies are predispositions. The predictable way we go about satisfying our emotional needs. When you call on *tendency action plays* (TAPs) to trigger and stimulate the other guy's highly predictable emotional needs, to trigger and stimulate the other guy's highly predictable emotional needs, you're *directing* rather than *confronting*. It's your argument's desired outcome that satisfies the needs you've triggered. Here's how to TAP into those needs:

TAP #1: "Fleeting Opportunity" Power

We have a need to get or see what will soon be gone.

When was the last time you visited a museum? If you're like me, it was probably to catch a temporary exhibit. Traveling museum exhibits (Fabergé eggs and the jewels of the Romanovs, for example) are more profitable and more popular than permanent exhibits that often are much more impressive. Viewers who haven't visited their museum's permanent exhibitions in years rush to see touring exhibits, knowing that they'll soon be packing up and hitting the road.

Auctioneers are masters of the "fleeting opportunity" tactic. Here's how a successful Los Angeles art auctioneer owned up to the secret of his success: "Make the auction go quickly. Keep the clock ticking. Keep the environment kinetic. Don't give bidders a lot of time to think between bids. Create a 'last chance' feeling that unless immediate action is taken, the item could be lost to another."

When I put on the khakis and leather laces, it's usually with a Hawaiian-style shirt. Shirts that remind me to kick back. Shirts so in-your-face colorful that I know the jacket-and-tie part of my week is over. I know my Hawaiian shirts. On Maui, every other shop sells Hawaiian shirts. The ones that don't sell Hawaiian shirts sell chocolate-covered macadamia nuts. The shirts and the nuts are my two island vices. As I was thumbing through a center-aisle shirt rack, the clerk pointed to a rack off to the side. "These patterns are flyin' out the door," he proudly declared. I knew better. Their flyin' days were over many luaus ago.

It was a jacket-and-tie day when I met with Scott, a successful home builder, in his Arizona office. A plaster topographic model of Scott's latest project showed prospective buyers where streets and houses would soon be built. Scott's model was dotted with itty-bitty trees, cars, greenbelts, and "sold" flags. "We really haven't sold this many houses," Scott confided as he pointed to the itty-bitty "sold" flags, "But this should heat things up."

"The X factor. It's the one unpredictable element that can put the ki-bosh on even the most brilliant of fleeting opportunity pitches. That factor is inertia," writes *Entrepreneur*.

Inertia is the propensity people have not to take action. It's possible that the other person may find your argument convincing, but not respond to your call for action for no reason other than sheer inertia. Hard to swallow, but true. Inertia is one of the most powerful phenomena in the world of influence.

The X Factor is the wall that magazine publishers hit when readers don't renew their subscriptions. Not because they no longer want the magazine, but because of the X Factor. Their antidote to the X Factor is the "promptness bonus"—the gift, extra issue, or special discount you earn by ordering or renewing within a specified time period. Don't overlook the X Factor. People by their nature are slow to change or take action. But what is rewarded gets done.

Tap into the other guy's need to take advantage of your argument's fleeting opportunities. And remember what is rewarded gets done.

TAP #2: Having "What's Hard to Come By" Power

"MEMBERS AND NON-MEMBERS ONLY."
–SIGN OUTSIDE THE MANDINGA DISCO IN MEXICO'S HOTEL EMPORIO

Scarcity imparts perceived value. Dorothy's ruby slippers from *The Wizard of Oz* sold for $165,000. The bullwhip used by Harrison Ford as Indiana Jones sold for $24,300.

A stash of 600 or so cigars was found in a cellar where Irish dampness kept them well preserved and smokable since the 1860s. The owner turned down an offer to sell all of them for $2,000 per cigar—$22 per puff, according to those in the know.

John F. Kennedy's walnut cigar humidor sold for $574,500. The body tag from Lee Harvey Oswald's corpse sold for $6,600. The estate of Jacqueline Kennedy Onassis was auctioned piece by piece by Sotheby's. The auction fetched stratospheric prices, prompting the scene to be dubbed "Camelot craziness." Intrinsic value played a small part in the frenzy. Jackie's diamond, ruby, and emerald necklace sold for $156,000. It was resold two years later—this time without the hoopla or hype—for $74,000, a 53 percent plunge from the stratosphere.

On New York's Madison Avenue, I saw a street merchant selling watches from a case resting on a collapsible stand. Two blocks away, another watch vendor was similarly fixturized for business. Most people walked by the first vendor without missing a beat, but stopped to glance at the second vendor's wares. The difference? The first vendor's watches were jammed together sardine style. The second vendor only had six watches on display. He had created an appearance of scarcity.

I had a few hours to kill before heading to the Las Vegas airport and home. Those few hours left me with two choices: gamble or shop. I opted for the shopping. Even pricey stores are a better bet than craps. I headed to the Ralph Lauren Polo store that was then in the Caesar's Forum Shops.

On an antique table in the middle of the store were five ties perfectly laid out side by side. They were the same except for the color of their stripes. A very different red-orange/bright-blue combination caught my eye. While standing at the cash register, I noticed the tie had a snag. "No problem," a salesperson said. "Let's go over to the tie drawer."

The open drawer revealed a chaotic jumble of about 40 striped ties. Many the same as the one I had chosen. She pulled a tie from the scramble and carefully smoothed it out. Too late. I was turned off the minute the drawer was pulled open. Before going to the tie drawer, my choice was unique, but now it was just another tie. All the smoothing out and tissue-paper wrapping in the world wasn't going to change that. How we look at everything in life—a New York street vendor's not-so-fine watches, Polo's fine ties, and your argument—is a matter of presentation.

I'm not alone in how I felt. Shopping mall stores find that by displaying fewer clothes, they encourage full-price purchases. They know that you'll be more willing to pay full price for a jacket you love if you see that there are only six of them on the rack.

And while we're on the fashion scene, remember the little green Lacoste crocodile? At one time the logo only appeared on the finest of cotton knit shirts. But then General Mills bought the Lacoste brand, and soon the croc was appearing on polyester schlock. By the mid-1980s, the logo had little cachet—the victim of overexposure on discounter's racks.

The Lacoste family came to the croc's rescue. The brand is back under their control. You may have trouble spotting the croc, though. He can only be spotted in the best of stores and only on the likes of expensive knit shirts and sweaters. The Lacoste family's save-the-croc strategy: make something less accessible and it becomes more desirable.

And now for some fashion news about the teensy-weensy black bikini: Chanel, the Paris fashion house, introduced the black "eye patch" bikini, named for the approximate area of breast coverage. Only the bikini is teensy-weensy. The tab: $500. When asked about the price, a Chanel publicist explained how special the bikini is, and that the price is based on the fact that you won't see every woman wearing it. Triumph, the Japanese lingerie-maker, celebrated soccer's World Cup with 100 limited edition bras with soccer-ball-printed cups. The $130 bras were a sellout.

Or consider baseball cards: Hockey Hall of Famer Wayne Gretzky sold his 1909 Honus Wagner baseball card for $1,270,000 on an Internet auction. It was one of an estimated 50 that remain. Another owner stated he would be glad to rent you his Honus Wagner for $100,000 a year. *Forbes* warned that the printing and paper don't justify the card's exalted status. Collecting baseball cards has never made sense as an investment. When you buy cards, you're buying inflated goods. You're hoping some other fool will come along and pay you even more.

It's called the "Coors Effect." There was a time when Coors beer was only available in parts of the West. Because people want what they can't get, a cult following for the beer developed on campuses elsewhere. East Coast students were known to drive hundreds of miles to buy a case of Coors. Years later when Coors became available nationwide, the Coors cult quickly evaporated, as Coors became just another easily gotten brew.

Krispy Kreme suffered the Coors Effect. In late 2000, a Krispy Kreme store opened in Rochester, New York. By 5 a.m., more than 100 people were lined up in a snowstorm to be among the first to get a sugary sweet doughnut hot off the conveyor belt. By 6 a.m., 75 cars were clogging the drive-through lane. The "newsworthy" event was played out on three television stations and live radio. The excitement was real—Krispy Kreme had come to Rochester. But Krispy Kreme grew so quickly that it soon lost its cult status. Today, you can buy the doughnuts at grocery stores, where you fill your gas tank, and in self-serve display cases. "Doughnut theater," where anxious customers watch behind glass as doughnuts are cooked and then splashed with white glaze, just isn't exciting "theater" anymore.

Tap into the other person's need to have what's not easily gotten. Create an aura of scarcity. What is hard to come by has a greater value than what is easily gotten. Availability is a yardstick of quality. It's what we can't get that we want most of all.

TAP #3: "Need to Reciprocate" Power

A couple you hardly know invites you to their daughter's June wedding. Your own daughter will be getting married over the Fourth of July weekend. Are you going to feel obligated to invite this couple to your daughter's wedding?

Years ago, my folks decided to sell their home and move in to a condo. They interviewed salespeople from the area's two largest realtors and were duly impressed by both. I recommended Jerry B., a young fellow who had just opened his own office. Mom and Dad liked Jerry, but they felt they would be better off with a more seasoned pro.

I was surprised to learn that Jerry did bag my folks' listing. Why did they change their minds? Jerry had a 6-foot salami delivered to them with a note that read: "No baloney, I'd really like your listing." Mom and Dad felt obligated to reciprocate by giving Jerry his chance. Jerry understood human nature and good deli. Yes, he sold the house. And yes, today he is one of the city's most successful real estate brokers.

You've heard this one before: *Knock. Knock.* "I've got a free gift for you!" Whether it's a door-to-door salesperson's "free gift" or an Amway product sampler, people who receive something for nothing feel an obligation to buy. When the Disabled American Veterans seek contributions through the mail, their response rate doubles if unsolicited gummed address labels are enclosed with the solicitation. Maybe this need to reciprocate is because of what we're taught early on: Only ingrates and the selfish take without giving back.

Tap into the other person's need to free himself from psychological debt by repaying it. Do something for the other guy because he's preprogrammed to reciprocate. He'll meet your concessions with concessions of his own. Use small favors to prompt large favors in return.

TAP #4: "Fulfilling Aspirations" Power

Nike's "Just Do It" ad took a full page:

All your life you are told the things you cannot do. All your life, they'll say you're not good enough or strong enough or talented enough. They'll say you're the wrong height or the wrong weight or the wrong type to play this or be this or achieve this. They will tell you no and *you will tell them yes.*

Reebok didn't have a full-page ad, but managed to say it all in just eight letters: "We let UBU."

People want to be the most of who they are. Take the U.S. Army's former recruiting slogan "Be All That You Can Be."

Calvin Klein ran ads for its unisex ck fragrance as part of its "Just Be" campaign. One ad read "Be a saint. Be a sinner. Just Be." Another ad read "Be bold. Be shy. Just Be." Still another read "Be a dreamer. Be a doer. Just Be."

In the United States, most women regularly shave to remove body hair. Not so in Europe, where attitudes about female hair removal vary from country to country. These attitudes are influenced by long-established cultural conditions and varying notions of beauty. So how did Gillette go about changing European women's belief that shaving is not just a man's work? Gillette's television campaign focused on vignettes of young women with "aspirational" lifestyles. One commercial had children on the beach caressing their pretty young mother's legs. By showing mothers what they *could be*, Gillette convinced them to reevaluate their deep-rooted attitudes about hair removal.

We live in a topsy-turvy world of job downsizing, making ends meet, and moral debates. We realize that our own personal aspirations and attitudes must be greater than the sum of our daily duties. More than ever, we need to be able to connect with ourselves. To overcome self-ambiguity. To better understand just who we are. Each of us struggles to make sense of our lives and to deepen our understanding of its purpose. When your argument appeals to a person's dream of what he or she can become, your ideas will take on new and powerful meanings.

Tap into the other person's needs to make better sense of who she is. Empower her to be who she is and who she wants to be. Show her how your suggestions can turn her aspirations into reality.

Godiva chocolates come in a gold box and are marketed as "the perfect gift." Its core market is women older than 35. To counter sluggish sales, the chocolate-maker launched an "aspirational lifestyle" campaign aimed at women between the ages of 25 and 35. Although the word *diva* in Italian means "goddess," in pop culture it's synonymous with pride and strength. Every woman aspires to be a diva. The new campaign plays off the brand name—Go*diva*. The chocolatier's advertising agency calls it a "you only live once" campaign, saying, "A diva feels that an indulgent lifestyle has been earned." The aspirational tag line: "Inside every female is a diva."

TAP #5: "Need to Catch a Wave" Power

Natural shoe polishes. Natural soft drinks. Natural stuff to change your natural hair color or bronze your natural skin tone.

It seems everyone was squeezing onto the "natural" bandwagon, even when the fit was an awkward one: Alberto VO5 "naturals shampoo" contained sodium chloride, phosphoric acid, sodium laureth sulfate, and so on. Aveeno Moisturizing Lotion "for natural relief of dry skin" contained phenycaribol and dimethicone. Clairol's Natural Instincts conditioning colorant came with a warning: "Caution: This product must not be used for dyeing the eyelashes or eyebrows; to do so may cause blindness."

Operation Desert Storm introduced us to "smart bombs." "Smart" was suddenly the bandwagon link-up word as a blitz of "smart" businesses came into being. The "Smart Chopper" smartly diced and sliced vegetables. "Smart Cuts" was the place to go for a smart hairdo. But there were also "Smart Systems," "Smart Choice," "Smart Creations," "Smart Start," "Smart Gym," "Smart Way," and the "Smart Yellow Pages."

And then there was the "value" bandwagon and commonly found link-up names: "Valu-Pak," "Valu-Plus," "Valu-Rite," and "value-added software." The "value" craze got so out of hand that the CEO of Taco Bell in exasperation declared in newspaper advertisements, "Value has become a consumer expectation—'value' this, 'value' that. Blah, blah, blah."

To rescue ourselves from the sameness of our days, we're quick to pick up on what is "extreme." New York phone company ads touted "Xtreme dialing" and even included a recipe for "Extreme Lemonade" (just add pineapple juice). Snickers candy bars are "extremely nuts." Playing to the magic of threes, the Suzuki X-90 was pitched as "xceptional. xciting. xtreme." Boston Market restaurants featured "Extreme Carver" sandwiches. Izod, a clothing manufacturer, pitched "Extreme Leisure" sportswear. "Extreme Investing" was a *Fortune* cover story. Clairol pitched XtremeFX hair color to teenage boys.

Our friends Mary and Ellen are college-educated, middle-aged women with grown children. They are smart. They are wise. And they have a true sense of what things are worth. So why is it that when we got together with them a few years back, the conversation turned to Tabasco the bull, Kiwi the toucan, Zip the cat, Weenie the dachshund, and Bronty the dinosaur? And how Curly, Valentino, Peace, Glory, Fortune, and the other bears are the hardest Beanie Babies to come by?

When the fuzzy little critters stuffed with beans first hit the market, they retailed for $5.99. A few years later, collectors were boasting ownership of Pinchers the lobster, estimated to be worth $3,000; Brownie the bear, worth $4,500; and Peanut the elephant, worth $5,000.

People started to believe that the reported prices were the actual value. Ty, Inc. had orchestrated a world-class marketing coup. Pulling different models off the market before the demand for that model was fully satisfied created a perceived collector's value. But as with all crazes, the price of Beanie Babies—including Princess, the teddy created in Princess Diana's memory—went into a free fall.

A *London Observer* article found striking similarities between Beanie Babies and the Dutch Tulip Mania.

In the 1630s, in one of the first financial manias on record, the price of tulip bulbs in Holland sky rocketed. At one point, you could trade a single tulip bulb for two stacks of wheat, four stacks of rye, four oxen, eight pigs, 12 sheep, two hogsheads of wine, four barrels of beer, two barrels of butter, 1,000 pounds of cheese, a bed, a suit of clothes, and a silver drinking cup. The Semper Augustus, a tulip bulb, sold for today's equivalent of $50,000.

And before anyone ever heard the words Beanie Baby....

By 1925, the automobile and airplane had put southern Florida within reach of anyone on the East Coast. Lured by the vision of a vast beachfront playground, speculators sent land prices skyrocketing. Lots in downtown Miami jumped $10,000 an hour some days. Armed with maps and deeds, real estate agents made sales while standing on street corners. It was only after visitors had gotten a taste of southern Florida summers (pre-air-conditioning) and a 1927 hurricane that left more than 400 people dead that the madness finally stopped.

A perceived wave can be as compelling as the real thing: an East Coast disco wanting a hottest-spot-in-town image pays fashionably dressed shills to stand in line outside its front door.

Tap into the other guy's preprogrammed need to lock-step with what's new and novel. Tune into fads, trends, and fashions. Link your ideas to what's hot—or perceived as hot.

TAP #6: "Need to Enhance Self-Image" Power

Maybe you're a lot like me. If I'm buying a gift that is the same price at Macy's as it is at Saks Fifth Avenue, I will go out of my way to buy it at Saks. You get a nice sturdy box, not one of those fold-up jobs. Tissue paper folded just so and sealed with a gold sticker, and a pretty hand-tied ribbon instead of one of those stretchy pretend ribbons. It's worth going out of my way because I like what buying at Saks says about me.

Self-image ads pitch tooth whiteners, shampoos, and exercise equipment. But here's how Slim-Fast pulled out all the self-image stops: Slim-Fast's largest potential market in Europe is the UK, where 38 percent of the population is overweight and where the idea of having a shake or bar replace a meal is a strange notion. To convince British women otherwise, Slim-Fast ads are tapping into their self-image insecurity by telling them to lose pounds or else lose face to their sexier counterparts in Sweden, Spain, and France. One ad is a photo of a French model with the caption "I love British women. They make me look great." Another ad has a Spanish model and the text "Face it, British women, it's not last year's bikini getting smaller."

To enhance their self-image, inner-city kids want boutique-chic fashion. Designer labels are what is termed "aspirational brands." Rap stars are given designer clothing to wear when appearing on stage. It's part of designers' marketing strategies to create demand for their label in urban culture.

Grey Goose vodka has become a top-seller despite its high price by portraying itself as the vodka of choice for wealthy people with impeccable taste. We think of ourselves as being rational. In truth, we are very emotional. Happiness comes from how we see ourselves. We act in ways that make us appear to both ourselves and others as competent and discriminating.

Premium "sticks"—handmade cigars containing only whole-leaf, "long filler" tobacco—have become a favored accessory for Demi Moore and Arnold Schwarzenegger. It was only natural that hand-rolled cigars have become a "cool tool" for the terminally hip or hip wanna-be.

Feeling a little down? The root of the problem may be on the top of your head, not in it. Frizzy, flyaway, lackluster hair results in low self-esteem, increased self-consciousness, and a loss of confidence. A bad hair day brings out social insecurities. It causes people to concentrate on their negative aspects, according to a Yale University psychology professor in her study with the stop-and-smile title "The Psychological, Interpersonal and Social Effects of Bad Hair."

Tap into the other person's need to act in ways that enhance how she sees herself having class, being hip, being discriminating, avoiding embarrassment, and possessing those qualities that magnify her sense of self-worth.

TAP #7: "Needing Recognition" Power

"In New York, you're nobody until a sandwich is named after you."
—The *Wall Street Journal*

Years ago, I was one of three guests invited to speak to a business group. The other two speakers were well-established and well-known.

Before our presentation, there was an informal wine and cheese reception. The arriving audience converged on the two other guests, asking them to autograph their books and answer questions. Unknown and un-noticed, I felt like Dolly Parton's ankles.

I helped Tommy Lee negotiate his departure from the legendary rock band Motley Crue. So why did Tommy leave? When it comes right down to it, maybe being a drummer in a rock 'n' roll band isn't so great after all. Unless, of course, you don't mind being hidden at the back of a stage, banging cymbals and pounding drums, while the singers and guitarists get the glory and recognition.

Tommy went public saying he "was starving for some attention." He had onstage cries for recognition: setting his drums on fire, hanging from bungee cords. He had that all-too-famous video of his honeymoon with Pam Anderson. But Tommy only got to step out front-and-center when he formed his own band. Tommy has achieved the recognition he quested for. He's now a singer/guitarist.

Tommy Lee and Andrew Carnegie on the same page! What they have in common is that the same lesson can be learned from each....

Through sheer savvy, Andrew Carnegie, a penniless immigrant, built Carnegie Steel, the core of what became U.S. Steel. In the process, he became the world's richest man. Here are a few examples of how Carnegie harnessed everybody's need for recognition and why he was "The Master Motivator."

J. Edgar Thomson was the president of the Pennsylvania Railroad. To capture the railroad's steel business, Carnegie went beyond the norm of wining and dining a potential customer. Instead, he employed a can't-fail recognition strategy: Carnegie built a giant steel mill in Pittsburgh and christened it the "J. Edgar Thomson Steel Works." From then on, the railroad's steel business was Carnegie's.

When Carnegie and George Pullman were engaged in a price war for control of the business of building train sleeper cars, Carnegie tried to convince Pullman that they should join forces. Pullman wasn't persuaded. Then Pullman asked, "What would you call the new company?" "Why, Pullman's Palace Car Company, of course," Carnegie quickly replied. Carnegie's recognition of the Pullman name clinched the merger.

When Royal Viking cruise ships sailed the seven seas, they were among the best of the best. As a cruise ship guest lecturer, I discovered some of Royal Viking's behind-the-scene secrets. The cruise line was famous for its onboard awards ceremonies. Elderly passengers wearing jewels and sequins from a social swirl gone by accepted awards simply for being on their 30th or 40th or 50th Royal Viking cruise. Why did they take so many cruises?

The ship's staff was coached to remember passenger names, to go out of their way, to listen, and then to listen some more. Single men in crested blazers earned free cruises by serving as "hosts" and schmoozing with passengers. Ship's officers in their 30s invited women with clouds of blue hair to dance. Social hostesses knew to admire formal jewelry and gowns. For many, Royal Viking was selling something the passengers needed more than an ocean voyage—recognition.

Carnegie and Royal Viking both understood that people are highly motivated by recognition.

Tap #8: "Social Norm" Power

We live in a world where our conduct is influenced by two dynamics: the social norm "do the right thing" dynamic, and the "it's business" economic dynamic. For most people it's a difficult balance.

Sometimes, my tactic is to request a concession by casting my request as an opportunity for the other person to do the right thing; to not take advantage of a situation although it would be legal to do so.

Len, a mortgage lender, foreclosed on our client Helen's house. At the foreclosure sale, title to the house changed from Helen to Len. Helen had made regular mortgage payments to Len for more than five years. But New Normal times were tough. As hard as she tried, she hadn't be able to make any payments for about four months.

We asked Len if Helen could live in the house for six more weeks rent-free. This way, her 10-year-old son, Jake, could finish his school year. Len's alternative was to opt for a speedy eviction.

I spoke to Len, who was one very tough businessman. The focus of my conversations with him was doing the socially right thing rather than Helen's failure to make payments as promised in her loan agreement. Luckily, Len's social conscious made it possible for Helen to stay in the house until the end of Jake's semester.

AARP asked lawyers if they would give legal assistance to needy retirees at a fraction of their regular hourly rate. The response was no. But later, when AARP asked the lawyers to offer their services for free, their response was an overwhelming yes.

When money was a dynamic, the lawyers compared the highly discounted rate to their regular hourly billing rate. They weren't prepared to take the hit. When volunteering, a *social norm* was the motivating dynamic. The lawyers' decision was based not on money, but on what was "the right thing to do."

Social norms are a source of *self-definition*: the type of person you are. The type of person you aspire to be. Social norms *motivate* acceptance of your concession requests when the other person is reminded that what he does defines his life values and who he is.

Tap into people's need for recognition. People act in ways that will gain them recognition. Show the other person recognition—a pat on the back, encouragement, a special treat—and your beliefs may become his beliefs.

Now Cinch Things With a Call for Action

Because it's now time to clearly say what it is you want

The evening news supplies information, but has little impact on public opinion. It doesn't ask viewers to change what they think. Winning an argument is not merely about presenting information. It's about persuasively *leading* others to your call for action.

Fill in this blank:

At the end of my argument, the thing I want to happen is _____.

Your answer is your call for action.

*"Isn't it true that the only time you have ever really benefited from anything in your life has been when you said yes instead of no?—*Motivational speaker Tom Hopkins' "power close."

Back in the neighborhood: Here's how you, when speaking at the "no multiplex" neighborhood meeting, could persuasively play your hand:

☐ *Grab the audience's attention: "We are at a crossroads, and I'm here to review some critical things I've discovered."*

☐ *Bond with the audience: "We all like going to movies, and we like the convenience of having theaters close by...."*

☐ *Present your core argument: "If a multiplex theater is built, our neighborhood will surely suffer...," and then present your three portable points.*

☐ *End with your call for action: "As your friend, as a concerned mother, and as a neighbor, I urge you to call Councilwoman Smith. Write to Mayor Jones. Attend the planning and zoning commission meeting Thursday evening. Tell the commission you won't tolerate a multiplex as your new neighbor."*

Let's Rewind

The call for action is made only after the speaker's argument is presented. If she starts with her call, her logic may not be heard. When someone tells you a joke, do you sometimes listen with only half an ear? Are your thought processes busy mentally rehearsing a joke that you'll share in return? So, too, we all instinctively prepare mental counterarguments the moment we know what the other fellow is arguing for.

The speaker's call has two critical elements: a sense of immediacy, and a very specific request. A general call is flabby and weak. ("If you agree with me, do something about it!") A winning call for action doesn't pussy-foot around.

Ronald Reagan was invited to speak at the Berlin Wall to help commemorate the city's 750th anniversary. He was cautioned not to make any Soviet-bashing, inflammatory statements about the Wall. Drafts of his speech were circulated to the State Department and the National Security Council for their review, and they were cautioned that any text too proactive would be an affront to Gorbachev. Their suggestion was for Reagan to say: "One day, this ugly wall will disappear."

The president stood at the Berlin Wall on June 12, 1987, and declared to the world, "Mr. Gorbachev, tear down this wall!" There it was. No hopeful thinking. No euphemisms. A clear, unequivocal call for action.

Have you noticed that the new wave of advertising doesn't pull any punches either…?

Advertisers have discreetly shielded consumers from what is really going on in the bathroom. Traditionally, they've called toilet paper "bathroom tissue," a phrase never used by anyone outside of Madison Avenue. Kleenex is now using the w-word. They advertise that their Cottonelle toilet paper *wipes* better than ordinary toilet paper.

And advertisers have discreetly shied away from telling us what may be in our bottled water. O Premium Waters, a small Arizona-based bottled water company, has changed all of that. Its regional television spots show two outdoorsmen urinating in a mountain stream. O Premium Waters' warning: "Do you know what's in your bottled water? Not everything is on the label."

Don't Hang the Meat so High the Dogs Won't Jump for It

That's how a Texas judge cautions litigants about arguing for an unreasonable objective. Your call for action should give you a real shot of winning something of true benefit. Cast and limit your call to what's *realistically obtainable*.

And now for a little *nun*sense to make my point….

First Take

Nun to Mother Superior: "Is it all right if I smoke while praying?"

Mother Superior (shocked): "Certainly not!"

Second Take

Nun to Mother Superior: "Is it all right if I pray while I'm smoking?"

Mother Superior: "Of course! It's always good to pray."

Let's say you want a raise. You're ready to meet with your boss and argue why you deserve more money. But wait a minute. Can you predict how your boss will probably respond? Is it likely she will respond, "I just don't have the budget to give raises this year"? If that's your prediction, what can you reasonably expect to gain by arguing for more money?

Now, ask yourself what is realistically obtainable: *Do I have a chance to move into a different position within the company? Do I have a chance for more training? How about an overseas assignment?*

Your call for action has to be clear and unequivocal. Your core argument states what you're arguing for (for example, no new multiplex). Your call for action is what you want others to do (for example, vote no, or write to your representatives).

My $50 Tip
Because silence is compelling

You've made your call for action. So far, no response? You'll want to say something. But don't. Whether you call it strategic patience, or watchful waiting, or disciplined inaction, or just being cool, quietly wait for the other guy to break the silence, and respond to you.

On the first night of a Baltic Sea cruise, my wife and I were assigned to a dining table with three other couples who were strangers to us. It was a friendly group. By the time dessert arrived, we knew where everybody was from, how many kids they had, and the kind of work they did.

Hugh, a rancher from Montana, asked about my persuasion and negotiation seminars. He then said, "Tell me your very best negotiating tip."

"That would be hard to do," I responded.

"I don't have time to go to one of your seminars, but I'll give you $20 cash, right here on the spot, if you spend two minutes telling me your very best piece of advice."

I smiled at Hugh, but said nothing.

"Okay," Hugh said. "Let's make that $50."

Hugh then slid two $20s and a $10 right alongside my cup of coffee. "No matter what you charge," he said, "on a per-minute basis this may be the best fee you'll ever get."

Hugh was right. And I picked up his cash.

"Hugh, here it is, my best piece of negotiating advice: There's magic in not opening your mouth."

"I don't understand."

"Hugh, did you notice how you raised your ante from $20 to $50 without my ever having said a single, solitary word?"

"Certainly you can embellish the advice a little if you're going to keep my $50."

"Well, in addition to not opening your mouth, you could try a quick shoulder shrug or a fast wince. Either one would throw a little *attitude* into the mix."

I now call the advice I gave Hugh "My $50 Tip."

You made your call for action. There is never a need to break the silence by answering your own questions, or filling a lull in a conversation, or, in Hugh's case, upping the ante by $30.

Return your mouth to its full upright position. Stop talking when you've made your call for action. You'll have an urge to talk. It is easier to manage sound than silence. Do not repeat yourself. Do not resell. Do not rephrase.

We mistakenly believe that the more we say, the more we influence. But probably nothing you can say will improve the silence. By anxiously sweetening your proposal before there is a response, you're only arguing against yourself.

If the response is a question, keep your answer short and to the point.

Meet Jay K.

Because he knows what I mean by "attitude"

After telling the story about Hugh to a group of MBA students, one of them asked, "What do you mean by 'attitude'?" Fortunately, her question followed on the heels of my college fraternity reunion. At our reunion banquet dinner, Jay K. got up to make "an announcement and a first-time confession." Jay lived in Chicago, but he wanted to go to Cal Berkeley. His secret: He never applied for admission. Jay just signed up for classes, completed enrollment forms, and attended classes as if he were accepted. Jay graduated with us, his secret intact. We all asked Jay, "How did you pull it off?" Jay shrugged his head sheepishly. "Attitude," he said. Jay's "and why not?" attitude, his optimistic mind-set, was he could and would attend and graduate from Berkeley even if it meant sneaking in the back door.

Chapter Summary

People act and react in highly predictable ways as they quest to satisfy their subconscious and conscious emotional needs—emotional needs to take advantage of fleeting opportunity, to have what is hard to come by, to return favors with favors, to fulfill aspirations. To do what's new and happening, to satisfy self-image, to be recognized by others for who we are and what we do.

Tendency action plays (TAPs) trigger and stimulate those emotional needs. Cinch consent by directing the other person to your desired outcome as a way of his satisfying the needs you've triggered.

With linkage and logic in place, it's time to be specific about what it is you want the other person to do, think, or see. That is your argument's call for action.

10

Throw a "Hail Mary"

Because it's never over till it's over

It's bound to happen. Not every argument will be guide-path smooth. There will be days filled with frustrating go-nowhere dead ends and exasperating drop-offs.

In this chapter, you'll discover how to artfully maneuver your way through the "mind-field."

Meet 3 Arguing Brothers

Because knowledge is important, but without creativity, knowledge has nowhere to go

A father and his three sons are traveling across a harsh desert.

Knowing he is about to die, the father summons his three sons to his side. "I have but 17 camels. To my eldest son I leave one-half of my camels. To my middle son, one-third of my camels. And to my youngest, one-ninth of my camels.

For years, the sons argued bitterly among themselves because 17 could not be divided by one-half, one-third, or one-ninth. One day a wise man said, "Let me loan you a camel." With 18 camels now to be shared, the eldest son took one-half, which was nine camels. The middle son took one-third, which was six camels. The youngest took one-ninth, which was two camels. The sons had collectively taken 17 camels (9 + 6 + 2). No longer needing the 18th camel, the sons returned it to the wise man.

Be a wise man and think outside the box. Seek solutions that aren't limited by the apparent or the assumed or by the fact there are only 17 camels to divide. The person who strikes first is admitting that his creativity is "on empty" and that he's run out of ideas.

Finesse *Worth*, *Value*, and *Share* Differences

Because it's easy when you know how

Many arguments are over quantitative *worth*, *value*, or *share* differences.

A common mistake is to become overly committed to your stated call for action—your announced position. Recall in Chapter 1 the fate of the African coastal monkey that won't let go of the peanut.

What if your call elicits a counter position? Without a still center, emotions and personalities wrongfully come into play. Defending your core argument becomes a matter of ego. Positional arguing without a strong fallback option is a risky game. A game you can sidestep by arguing for an *approach* rather than a *position*.

An approach can mean the difference between resolving a dispute and going to the mats. These six sure-fire, fast-acting, deadlock-busting approaches can be used in a variety of situations and ways.

Deadlock Buster #1

I had negotiated the sale of a hilltop mansion in Beverly Hills. However, during the pendency of the sale, a $1-million price reduction was argued for because the geological integrity of part of the property was put in issue. The parties' experts disagreed as to the seriousness of the potential that part of the lot could, unless supported, break away and fall down the hill. One thing was certain: The seller wanted to sell and the buyer wanted to buy. What could be done to resolve this conflict?

An argument avoiding *approach* was suggested. The two geologists would themselves choose a third geologist. The conclusion of this third geologist would be deemed controlling.

Consultants are called upon to settle executive salary disputes. Appraisers are often called on external criteria to resolve conflicts involving everything from antiques to business goodwill. Sometimes the deadlock, busting authority is a published reference. The Abos Marine Blue Book has the retail and wholesale value of boats. Kelley's Blue Book has the value of cars.

Deadlock Buster #2

To decorate their Turtle Creek, Texas, mansion, clients "T" and "R" acquired four fine oil paintings of slightly varying value. Later they decided to call it quits and no longer collect art or live together. They were arguing. What would be the best way to divide this art, realizing that each painting has a special value beyond its extrinsic worth?

It was agreed one person would get their first and fourth choices; and the other, their second and third choices. If they couldn't agree on who gets which set of choices, a flip of the coin would decide.

Deadlock Buster #3

An actress and her production company employer were deadlocked over an appropriate salary for the fourth season of a very successful soap opera. How could this deadlock be overcome?

Both the actress and the company would write down their final position—how much they would pay or agree to accept. If the two figures were within 15 percent of each other, they would be averaged. If they were more than 15 percent apart, a neutral party would select the more realistic figure of the two submitted. (This deadlock buster is often called "Baseball.") This approach encourages both sides to be reasonable in the formulation of their final offers.

Deadlock Buster #4

As an alternative approach to the one in Deadlock Buster #3, the neutral party could write down what she or he believed was the fairest and most equitable salary. That figure would not be disclosed to either the actress or her production company, who would then write down their own final positions. The position closest to the neutral party's figure would be the salary for the upcoming season. (This deadlock buster is often called "Golf.")

Deadlock Buster #5

"L" and "A" are in the midst of a divorce. Both worked for years building the family landscaping business. Each wants to buy the other's one-half interest in the business for as little as possible. They agree on only one thing: A stranger wouldn't pay top dollar for their business. How can they break this impasse and stop arguing?

One spouse (the "deciding spouse") would decide what would be both a fair price and fair payment terms for a one-half interest. The other spouse would then get to choose whether to be the buyer or the seller of that one-half interest, using the deciding spouse's price and terms.

The deciding spouse, not knowing whether he or she would be buyer or seller, would set parameters that would be realistic and fair to either side. If the role of the deciding spouse can't be agreed on, then the flip of a coin would be determinative.

Deadlock Buster #6

Jane owned a champion female Irish Wolfhound. Jane knew little about dog breeding, the care of a pregnant bitch, or what to do with a newborn litter. Paul, an experienced breeder and a new acquaintance, owned a champion male, the father of the litter. It was agreed that the litter would be shared equally.

The problem standing in the way of true romance was Jane's concern that Paul, with his superior expertise, would choose the best puppies for himself, leaving Jane with the less-desirable offspring. No one else in the state knew as much about Irish Wolfhounds as Paul. How could Jane avoid being at Paul's mercy?

It was decided that Paul would select two pups at a time. Jane would then select one of the two pups chosen by Paul for herself. Not knowing which pup Jane will select, with each draw Paul will pick the two pups with greatest championship potential with each draw.

Change to a More Friendly Level of Authority
Because sometimes it's the only way

Each level of authority has *people* who have their own needs for achievement, self-worth, and security. Each level has different individual roles to play out and different constituencies to court.

When Thomas Watson, Jr. was IBM's chairman, he called a meeting of his top executives to remedy what he considered to be a pressing problem. The problem was a complaint from an employee who found just the right *level* to make his argument: The employee had written to Watson's mother complaining that employees were not being treated fairly.

Turning to different levels of authority—the store manager instead of the store clerk, the store owner instead of the store manager—will expose different *level interests* and different *people interests*, and therefore different *patterns of resistance*. It is at the top where you will always find the greatest flexibility. The top has the risk-takers. The policy-makers. The people who are so secure in their positions that they understand the exceptions as well as the rules.

You're going nowhere when you argue to the *wrong people* about the *right thing*....

An evangelist returned home after a week of tent meetings. His wife greeted him by asking him how his sermons went. "Well," he replied, "all week long I was at my persuasive best. My sermon on Monday about charity was very well-received as was my sermon about salvation on Tuesday, holiness on Wednesday, and forgiveness on Thursday."

"What about Friday's sermon?" his wife asked.

"On Friday, I told how it was both a privilege and an obligation for the rich to give to the poor. My talk was passionate and enthusiastically received, but alas, it was all for nothing."

"I don't understand, how could that be?"

"The assembly of worshippers was very poor," he explained.

Meet Giorgio

Because rejection is a reactive response

Sometimes the resonse to your argument will be one word: no. *No* means the arguing-back-and-forth door is shut. It doesn't mean maybe. It means "I'm not interested in what you have to say."

Rejection of your argument is also a negative response. But the good news is that, by definition, a response means the lines of communication are still open.

Rejection doesn't exist in the abstract. Rejection is reactive. Remove what's causing the other person to reject your idea, and you've eliminated the problem.

A rejected point or proposal can be presented again and again as long as it appears fresh and new. When I boil spaghetti at home, it comes out either too hard or too mushy. But a restaurateur friend, Giorgio, makes perfect spaghetti. For years, Giorgio insisted that I'd never be able to make truly great spaghetti because my last name didn't end in *i* or *o*. I now know better. Giorgio's secret is to take a *spago* (single strand of spaghetti) from the boiling pot and throw it against a wall. When the spago sticks to the wall, it means your spaghetti is perfecto.

Family. Friends. Bosses. Coworkers. You want your link-up to be so comfortable and easy that you can keep throwing ideas and thoughts against the wall until something sticks. Call it the Art of Hanging In.

Deal with rejected points one bit at a time. Break big problems into smaller problems that can be reckoned with individually. Separate monetary and nonmonetary segments, discussing nonmonetary first.

Rejection is overcome by advancing your argument with a positive attitude and a soft touch. Hang in by recasting your suggestions so they appear fresh. Remember: Even creative nagging is still nagging.

You Can Run Though a Stone Wall

Because here are 5 keys to open the wall's door

When you're stonewalled, the other person is refusing to have a meaningful dialogue—the lines of communication are slammed shut. If you ask questions that begin with *can*, *can't*, *is*, or *isn't*, chances are you'll get a single-word response. Single-word answers don't supply insight into the other person's desires, perceptions, and needs. They don't tell us why he is resistant.

The keys to making that rock talk are *probing questions* designed to flesh out the concerns and motivator buttons of people who are otherwise unwilling to open up. Questions that can't be answered with the shake of the head or a single word such as *yes*, *no*, or *never*.

To ensure you neither prompt an argument nor appear confrontational, probing questions should be asked with a still center in a sincere, unhurried manner.

Key #1: Questions that aren't questions

Partial paraphrasing "questions" are not questions at all. Through this play, information is elicited by paraphrasing the speaker. Consider the following dialogue:

Person A: Things are crazy down here, and I won't be able to fill your order on Friday.

Person B: You won't be able to fill my order on Friday? (paraphrased response)

Person A: Well, we have this important job that takes priority.

Person B: Another job takes priority? (paraphrased response)

Person A: Your materials are in. But there is a bonus if we get this other job out early." (a previously hidden agenda is revealed)

To find out what happened to his order, Person B (the listener) partially paraphrased what Person A (the speaker) had already said.

Key #2: "What," not "why"

Why elicits a general "because" response. *What* produces a more specific response that better reveals true needs and interests.

Why questions are intimidating and prompt a defensive response:

Person A: That is my final decision.

Person B: *Why?*

Person A: Because I said so, that's why.

By contrast, *what* questions elicit fresh information on which new solutions may be based:

Person A: That is my final decision.

Person B: *What* are the reasons it is your final decision?

Person A: The reasons are….

Or:

Person A: I'm really too jammed to start a new project now.

Person B: Under what circumstances would you be able to start a new project?

Person A: I can't do it now, but maybe in a few weeks?

Key #3: "What if?"

What if questions pose *soft-touch* hypothetical possibilities. They aren't offers to be accepted or rejected, but rather questions to be answered. *What if* questions stimulate conversation while also supplying new information and insight into the other person's interests and goals. ("What if I was willing to wait until February to have you start my project?")

Key #4: Statement questions

Too many probing questions can make even the friendliest dialogue sound like an inquisition. *Statement questions* are probing questions disguised as statements. With some luck, the right lighting, and a little makeup, they'll not be recognized for what they really are.

Example #1: I was wondering what you thought of my proposal. (Question: What did you think of the proposal?)

Example #2: Although this makes a lot of sense to me, it may not seem like a good idea to you. (Question: What do you think of this idea?)

Key #5: "What will it take to convince you?"

"What will it take to convince you that now is the time to move…ours is the right company to do your job…my offer is both competitive and fair?"

Stone walls are often built because of the other person's negative expectations. Manage those expectations by telling her what she *expects*, *wants*, and *needs* to hear—and then, if possible, take action that is contrary to those expectations. *Expectation management* meant my telling a restaurant client's produce vendor what they needed to hear if they were to continue extending credit:

Example: "I know my client has not been the most dependable or reliable of customers. However, he now has the management and capital necessary to operate efficiently and to pay your bills timely."

Pounding on a stone wall with more of what wasn't working to begin with will only provoke more resistance. Why smash down walls when you have the keys to the door?

What if your Hail Mary pass doesn't work? I learned a long time ago that there is no sense to keep arguing with someone who hasn't any sense. And you can call that game "Hard Ball." But never slam the door closed—you may want to try opening it again.

To keep the door open, stay agile as you gather information. Neither reply nor confront too quickly. Rather than focusing on who's right, focus on who thinks what and why. Here are some answers to stay agile:

❒ "I don't know why you said that, so I'd like to know the reasons behind it."

❒ "We both know that Joe is smart enough (or too smart) not to realize that…."

❒ "Can you tell me more about what you just said?"

❒ "I would like to think about your comments."

❒ "Who put that in your mind?"

❒ "What is your objective here?"

❒ "Why don't we try to approach this in a more positive way?"

P.S: Never let 'em see you sweat.

Chapter Summary

It's never over until it's over. When you're able to "hang in," you can explore imaginative approaches and pose surgical strike questions (see Chapter 8).

Rejection is a response to something you or someone else has said or done. Rejection is finessed by dealing with that "something." Stone walls have doors that can be unlocked when you have the five keys.

If all else fails, do what Tom Watson's emplyee did. Change resistance levels.

Finesse Consent From Family and Friends

Because long-term relationships deserve special care and handling

In this chapter, you'll discover the way to win long-term results and preserve relationships that you can't turn your back on. So here it is, a self-persuasion strategy to finesse family, friends, and coworkers.

Recall meeting Sue, the daughter who argues nightly with her parents about homework? Let's continue where we left off in Chapter 6.

Your argument can threaten, bribe, plead, cajole, intimidate—plays that won't cause Sue to change. Studying just to make Mom and Dad happy isn't change. Sue will only truly change when it's in her self-interest to change. When *she wants* to adopt a new attitude about schoolwork; when *she believes* it's important to study.

Self-persuasion takes some effort, but it is a long-lasting, relationship-enhancing strategy. Pretend that Sue is your daughter. Now let's put a self-persuasion strategy into play.

Play #1: With a *still center*, consider the relationship at stake.

Sue is your daughter and she'll be your daughter for the long run. Assume there's an equality in your relationship with Sue. Agreed, there's a true difference in standing between a parent and a child, a boss and an employee, a teacher and a student. But a self-persuasion strategy is advanced by assuming a *fictional equality*. It's a state of equality that creates a *connectivity* that gives Sue the time and space to express her ideas and feelings. This state of fictional equality helps construct a *Consent Zone* where ideas can be tested and communications restored.

Use the Question Sandwiches and the 75/25 Partnering Secret in Chapter 3 to ensure that Sue has the space to make herself truly heard. Having been heard, Sue will be more receptive to what you have to say.

A fictional equality means resisting your urge to be…

❐ Diagnosing: "Sue, I know just what your problem is."

❐ Judging: "Sue, that's the craziest (or silliest, worst, most stupid) idea I've ever heard."

❐ Preaching: "Sue, you really should be…."

❐ Disparaging: "Sue, you're still only a kid and you don't understand."

❐ Minimizing: "Sue, you're trying to make a big deal out of it. Well, it's not."

It's important to the *persuasion progression* to hear Sue out. Try to understand how she feels. Show her you understand what it is she's telling you.

By identifying with Sue and her situation, she'll begin to feel that you'll try to work with her side-by-side rather than toe-to-toe. By *affecting* and *being affected*, you're creating an aura of *interactive power*. When Sue perceives you as sharing the homework/social life dilemma, your suggestions will be given a "teammate's" consideration:

Example #1: Your friends are very important to you. And I understand you feel like a study nerd whom life is passing by.

Example #2: I know you feel that your teachers really seem to be loading on the homework. They may not be aware of how many assignments each is giving you. But we need to talk about how the work will get done.

Play #2: Use *"I feel" statements* to express how you feel and what you want.

"I feel" statements are a *linking tactic* because they are not judgmental and can't be disproved.

Because you want Sue to understand your feelings and reasoning, what you don't want to say is "You're not studying enough...."

Example #1: I *feel* it's important that you study more because....

Example #2: I *feel* that high school is really a small part of life. We all have to make short-term sacrifices for long-term goals.

Sue can't find fault with your feelings. If you tell Sue you *feel* happy, she can't tell you you're wrong. If you tell Sue you *feel* sad, she can't correct you. How can Sue tell you that those aren't your feelings?

Chances are pretty good that you have a shopping list of grievances unrelated to Sue's studying: Her room is messy...her makeup is too heavy...her ears have been pierced one too many times. Now isn't the time to unload old baggage.

Avoid absolutes such as *always* and *never*. They beg for rebuttal. Rarely will anyone *always* or *never* do a given thing.

Be current with your specifics. Focus on how you want things done now. Don't look back to find fault. It may make you feel good to say your piece ("Why can't you do a good job like your brother does?"), but low blows will only make things worse.

Play #3: Tell Sue that your disagreement is with what she *does*, not who she *is*.

Now is the time to restate your positive feelings about Sue as a person. Empower Sue by letting her know that you're willing to explore mutually acceptable alternatives.

Example: I know that your friends are very important to you. And I think you know how strongly I feel about schoolwork.

Create hypothetical experiences. "Suppose we were..." or "Let's assume..." hypothetical experiences cause involvement. Involvement is the persuasive forerunner to change.

Quest for points of agreement rather than an overall solution. Moving from agreement to agreement rather than conflict to agreement is an *approach pattern* that will increase rapport and lessen Sue's resistance. If you can't agree on specific major issues, seek an agreement in principle that can be a bridge to further discussion.

Play #4: If a solution can't be reached, let Sue know that she's leaving you no choice other than to lay down study rules.

It's rare that someone will admit that he or she is being unreasonable. Asking Sue "Why can't you be reasonable?" or "What is your problem?" are questions that weaken linkage and invite further argument.

Act in a self-assured manner. Don't be defensive and don't apologize for your requests. Statements such as "I really don't like asking you to do this, but…" forecast and prompt a negative response. A *still center* keeps you from projecting weakness that would encourage Sue to become more forceful and domineering.

By casting your warning as a question rather than an edict, you'll be less likely to draw a combative response:

You think you should be able to be with your friends and do the things that are important to you. I feel that although studying requires time and effort, the long-term benefits are worth the sacrifice you need to make. If you won't study, what choice will I have other than to set rules and have penalties if they aren't followed?

Play #5: If Sue is willing to study harder, motivate her with praise.

The better Sue feels about how she's doing, the more motivated she'll be to succeed. Don't save the praise for As. Let her know that you appreciate how hard she is trying:

Example #1: I really like the way you started your homework on time today without arguing.

Example #2: That paper you did on the Revolution was excellent.

Play #6: If Sue isn't willing to study harder, firmly assert your position.

Being assertive is saying what you mean and meaning what you say. It's your clear *call for action*, and leaves no doubt where you're coming from.

Example #1: Sue, until your grades improve, everything else will have to take a backseat to study time.

Example #2: In this house, homework is your first priority. There will be no more arguments. You will do your homework and you will do the very best job you can do.

The difference between being aggressive and being assertive is sensitivity. Being aggressive is "being impossible back." ("I'm sick of wasting my time trying to get you to do your homework. Can't you ever do anything the way you're supposed to?")

Let's play out the scenario....

Mom: It's time to do your homework.

Sue: I need to call Josh to tell him what happened to me today. Just one more phone call...I promise.

Mom: It's always one more phone call. One more TV program.

Sue: You're not being fair! I'm losing all my friends because of you. Why are you always on my case?

Mom: Why shouldn't I be on your case? All you ever do is talk on the phone or watch TV. I'll be plenty fair when your grades improve!

Sue: Why are you always picking on me? Why can't you just leave me alone? It's not fair!

Mom, when you lost your still center you got in your own way and lost control. Did you feel the focus shifting from Sue's responsibility to study to whether you're being fair? Sue has lured you into an argument. That argument isn't even about homework anymore. It's now about fairness.

To avoid an argument with Sue, repeat your expectation firmly and clearly no matter what Sue says:

Mom: I understand. But I want you to do your homework now.

Sue: I need to call Josh to tell him what happened to me today. Just one more phone call...I promise.

Mom: I understand. But I want you to do your homework now.

Sue: You're not being fair! I'm losing all my friends because of you. Why are you always on my case?

Mom: I understand. But I want you to do your homework now.

Sue: Why do you always pick on me? Why can't you leave me alone? It's not fair!

Mom: I understand. But I want you to do your homework now.

You've avoided an argument by standing your ground. You were neither defensive of your position nor critical of Sue's.

If this stuck-in-a-groove play doesn't work, then it's time to back up your words by stating clearly and specifically what you mean and what will happen:

Mom: The decision is yours. Each night until you do your homework there will be no TV. No phone calls. No music. It's entirely up to you.

Cast your threat with caution. Meaningless, vague threats are worthless. ("You'll do your homework and you'll do it right or you'll be one very sorry young lady!")

Sue may try to manipulate you through anger, tears, or pleading. Be consistent. Back down and your credibility will be lost. And as for making a last-resort threat? Follow the rules in Chapter 6 (see page 92).

Chapter Summary

People who feel they're being talked into something can't be influenced. Self-persuasion plays make Sue feel you're working with her, side by side, affecting and being affected. A self-persuasion argument produces long-term, relationship-enhancing results.

Win the War of Words in Writing

Because sometimes writing your argument is the only way, and sometimes it's the winning way

Reports. Memos. Letters. Putting your thoughts in writing enables your reader to reread, to absorb, and to understand—luxuries listeners don't have. We write hoping that we'll be read. But you never really know if you'll be read, or if the reading will be anything more than a fleeting, light, once-over.

In this chapter you'll discover the secrets of how to write an argument that will be read.

Meet Mrs. Townsend

Because it's time for you to be set free

Upright and proper, Anna Townsend referred to herself not as our English teacher, but as a "teacher of English." God forbid that anyone would mistakenly think she was a teacher from England.

"The King's English." That's what Wilson High School's Anna Townsend called it. I called it "excruciating"—the tyranny of the pluperfects, those horrible predicates, the intransitives, split infinitives, gerunds, participles, and subjunctives. Be honest: Have you ever met anyone who claims grammar was their best subject? Or their favorite?

Mrs. Townsend's labyrinth of rules were the rules of formal expression. She had a say-it-my-way-or-no-way attitude about English. A lot of high school reunions later, I realize that Mrs. Townsend's rules are a framework, not a mandate.

From the time we have our first cup of coffee until we go to bed at night, we are assailed by persuasive writing of every kind and description. You write hoping you'll be read. Writing that does get read has a style that pulls readers in, not shuts them out. Style that is expressive. Imaginative. Style that allows your personal touch to shine through. It's all possible because today's King's English is the English of Larry King, Don King, Stephen King, Martin Luther King, and B.B. King.

Okay, I've set you free. But come-as-you-are found freedom isn't a license to wear sweats to the wedding. The written word will always be a little more formal than the spoken. But it's not the end of the world to begin a sentence with *but* or to end a sentence with a preposition. Or to even have sentences that aren't really sentences. You know. Those things Anna Townsend called "fragments." You don't have to get all worked up over *who* versus *whom* and *like* versus *as*. You're not getting graded and you won't be sent to grammar re-education camp.

Create a Hi-Touch Link-Up

Because convincing writing is convincing conversation in print

Arguments presented intellectually don't build trust. Trust is a reader's "good vibes" emotional response to how you are. Writers talk to readers. Let your ear guide your writing. Convincing writing is convincing conversation in print.

It's the "Does this sound like me?" test: Use words that real people use in real conversation. Advertisers hype their products as being robust, zesty, hearty, tangy. But has any conversation in your house ever sounded anything like this:

Person A: "Honey, what did you think of lunch?"

Person B: "The fruit drink was tangy, the salad dressing really zesty, and the stew was sure hearty, Dear."

We talk to each other in an active voice. When talking, you wouldn't say, "It is recommended by our councilwoman that we unite in opposition to the multiplex." You'd say, "Our councilwoman recommends...."

Before writing, take the time to think about what you'd say if you and your reader were arguing one-on-one. Now, say to yourself out loud what you would say if you were arguing face-to-face.

Quickly write down exactly what you said. You'll find yourself verbalizing emotions and thoughts that you wouldn't have otherwise put on paper. Don't correct your grammar. Don't move your words around. Just write down what you said, word-for-word.

It's only when you've run out of ideas that it's time to thumb through your notes. Some of the ideas that sounded good will come across as duds on paper. Toss those ideas out. Not all ideas will make your cut list.

Here's the hard part: not giving into your temptation to change vocabulary. Sure, formal words may better express your point, but they may also leave your argument sounding stuffy or pretentious. A radio advertiser claims it can give you the "verbal advantage" because a "powerful vocabulary gives a powerful impression." But winning arguments don't come from talking down to the other guy. Your goal is to win, not to impress.

Use small, mainstream words when you can. If a long word says just what you want to say, do not fear using it. But know that our tongue is rich in crisp, brisk, swift, short words. Make them the spine and the heart of what you say and write.

Will short words make you sound like a fourth-grade dropout? Decide for yourself. The quoted paragraph that you just read, from Richard Lederer's *The Miracle of Language*, is crafted almost entirely of one-syllable words! And here's a power-up plus: Words with the same meaning become more powerful as the number of syllables decreases 4-3-2-1. Which words in each line do your find most powerful?

Debilitate > undermine > weaken > sap

Accumulate > assemble > gather > stack

Erroneous > fallacious > faulty > wrong

Power up with "fireplug words"—short, punchy, graphic, to-the-point utility words. Which of these brims with power?

Take 1: A bear cub knocked everything off the shelf, tore our sleeping bags, and left the tent a mess.

Take 2: A bear cub trashed our tent.

In Take 2, 18 words were reduced to six by using the commonly understood fireplug word trashed. By dropping 12 words, a soggy sentence became crisp and memorable.

Would you call this award-winning writing? "Please read these materials so that you'll know what we plan to do at the meeting." This sentence is from a Ford Motor Company shareholder proxy statement. The statement's simplicity and the conversational quality of the accompanying letter from Ford's chairman won the automaker the Michigan Bar's annual Clarity Award.

Oh, if you're still worried that you'll sound like a dropout, try saying, "I'm just not the sesquipedalian I once was" (a long word meaning someone who is into long words).

How to Grab a Reader's Attention

Because you want to create an undertow

Whether your argument is part of a report or memo, or a stand-alone letter, you want your argument to grab interest and create an undertow that will sweep the reader down the page.

To get their attention, you have to hit people with a two-by-four. Subtle just doesn't work anymore. It's true.

Opening words should pop with energy: "You may think you're Jesus, but I know you're not because you wear glasses" (from a client's letter to her congressman who had a "preachy" attitude).

Will your writing be one of many that will be received? "One way to pull away from the crowd is to use sarcasm," advises *California Lawyer* magazine. "If a paragraph is an unusual experience, it will carry its point."[1] "Does pink make you puke?" That's the leading question in an advertisement for Urban Decay, whose nail polishes are a far cry from traditional pinks and reds.

How do you convince the 79 percent of men and 42 percent of women who presently don't wash their hands properly after using the bathroom to start practicing basic hygiene? (Their mothers' nagging didn't seem to work, so that's out as an option.) You start by grabbing their attention.

In an attempt to do just that, the Allegheny County, Pennsylvania, Health Department found a way to grab people's attention and at the same time educate them to the real potential harm not washing their hands has on themselves and others. How? By tweaking the opening lines of famous literature and posting the results on public restroom stalls. Some off-the-wall samples:

> "It was the best of times, it was the worst of times, it was the age of wisdom, it was the age of foolishness...it was the era of people not washing their hands after using the bathroom, it was the era of people eating with their hands and falling violently ill after transferring bacteria to each other. In short, it was not a very sanitary period."

> "Scarlett O'Hara was not beautiful, but men seldom realized it when caught by her charm....Scarlett had frivolously not washed her hands after attending to her business in the ladies' parlor.... Her delicate hands, being so unguarded...causing the unfortunate spread of an atrocious bacterial disease...."

Would Allegheny County's hygiene argument have been as effective if it had simply posted signs saying, "Be healthy. Wash your hands."?

How to Sculpt and Shape What You've Written

Because the less you write, the more people will remember

The Ten Commandments are 173 words long. Abraham Lincoln's Gettysburg Address is 266 words long. How many words are in the argument you've written? No one needs to tell you that ours is a hurry-up, just-tell-me world. Be direct. Did you over-inform or over-educate? The more filler and fluff you eliminate, the more likely your argument will get through.

Did you write things that are interesting, but not relevant? The executive director of a local charity wanting Bloomingdale's to put on a fashion show fund-raiser sent this solicitation letter to the Bloomingdale's CEO:

"Please find enclosed the materials that I promised you in my letter of last week. I apologize for the delay in getting these to you, but the office building out of which we work experienced a small fire on Tuesday. No damage was done to our actual offices, but our computer system was adversely affected for a few days."

Do you think the CEO really cared about the fire...or the amount of damage to the charity's offices...or what happened to the charity's computer system?

And did you write things that are relevant but not interesting? My wife and I will often take a guided tour on our first visit to a foreign city. It's our way of getting a quick handle on what the city is all about. It doesn't matter what the country—tour guides the world over launch into excruciating detail about events and people that no one on the tour really cares about. By the time the tour ends, we've forgotten most of what we heard—overdosed on detail.

I was putting the finishing touches on this chapter while vacationing "down under." A tour of the city of Christchurch included a visit to its botanical garden. Our guide's who-the-heck-cares tidbit: "Enoch Barker was the first Government Gardener of New Zealand." Ho hum. That was in 1863.

To carve his famous statue of David, it is said Michelangelo took a block of marble and chiseled away anything that didn't look like David. Here are three clutter cuts to sculpt away anything that doesn't look like it will advance your argument.

Cut #1: What is the point of all this?

Scrap the folklore and frou-frou. Let your personal style shine through—but too much is too much.

Cut #2: What's in it for the other guy?

Edit out anything that goes purely to your own self-interest. Sure, you can make your appeal to a man's better nature, but he may not have one. A *bulletproof argument* tells the other guy the payoff in it for him.

Cut #3: Are you telling the other person what he already knows?

Telling a listener or a reader what is obvious is a drag. How many times a day do you suffer through this example:

Hello, this is John Jones. I can't answer my phone right now because I'm either on another line or away from my desk. Please leave your name, the date and time you called, your phone number, any message, and the best time to call you back. I'll call you back as soon as I can.

Cutting out the obvious reduces this message from 55 to 18 words:

Hello, this is John Jones. I'm not able to take your call. Please leave a message. Thank you.

Even better is Joann Smith's voice mail: *This is Joann Smith. But enough about me.* Beep sound prompting caller to leave message.

Okay, every rule has its exceptions. And here are the four exceptions to the "Get on With it Already" Rule:

1. When you're cranking out an argument as part of a college term paper with a minimum page requirement.

2. When you're telling a compelling story as part of your persuasive pitch.

3. When too brief is simply too brief:

   The *Eskimo Cookbook's* recipe (in its entirety) for boiled owl:

   1. Take feathers off.

   2. Clean owl and put in cooking pot with lots of water.

   3. Add salt to taste.

4. When super "overkill" best hammers home your message.

On episodes such as "Your Love Is Mine!" and "Explosive Betrayals!" *Jerry Springer Show* guests have been known to strip down to their underwear and divulge their most intimate secrets. Do you have even a smidgen of a doubt as to how columnist Mike Downey feels about the show when he argues that it is "...the most repulsive, rotten, slimy, dirty, disgusting, vile, grotesque, stinking, depraved, demented, dreadful, putrid, rancid, appalling, shameless, heartless, mindless, worthless, cruel, crude, creepy, nasty, sleazy, sickening piece of filth in the history of American television."[2]

How to Advance in a Linear Progression

Because winning arguments pass the "Moving Forward" Test

Each sentence and paragraph needs to say something different from the one that preceded it. When reasoning is repeated, readers become confused and lose interest.

You'll have an urge to repeat points believing that if they're important, they're deserving of repetition. But repetition signals that there probably isn't much new up ahead. Whenever you write "in other words" or explain your explanation, you're really saying "Sorry, but I didn't do a very good job of getting my point across the first time."

Mrs. Townsend circled go-nowhere-tangents in red, saying they were "detours." Bulletproof reasoning moves forward without deviating and digressing. Steer clear of detours by tying each sentence to a prior sentence and each paragraph to a prior paragraph. Examples of tying words: *further, besides, first, when, however, conversely, as a result, for example, even so, finally.*

Arguments that pass the Moving Forward Test present background information in a cause-and-effect or chronological order. Points in strongest-to-weakest order. They limit each paragraph to just one idea or one point, and limit paragraphs to seven or eight lines at most. Don't be timid about using a one-sentence paragraph if it helps get your idea across.

How to Make Your Words Flow

Because you need to sweep the reader down the page

Arguments that flow make the easiest reading. Read aloud what you've written. Do the words flow easily across your tongue? When they do, you're on a winning track. Words should have a rhythm and sound good together. Breaks within a sentence should come at a natural point. When your words are read aloud, where will your reader pause for breath?

The inaugural ceremony is a defining moment in a president's career. John Kennedy wanted his address to be short and clear. (The final draft was 14 minutes long.) Though his colleagues submitted ideas and drafts, the final product was distinctly the work of Kennedy himself. Aides recount that every sentence was worked and reworked until it was listener- and reader-friendly. The climax of his speech was its most memorable phrase: "Ask not what your country can do for you. Ask what you can do for your country." A phrase that became more compelling and less clumsy than an earlier draft that said, "Ask not what your country is going to do for you...."

These drafts of the speech from the archives of the John Fitzgerald Kennedy Library show how he crafted his trip-easy address:

First Draft	Next-to-last Draft	Final Draft
We celebrate today not a victory of party but the sacrament of democracy.	We celebrate today not a victory of party but a convention of freedom.	We observe today not a victory of party but a celebration of freedom.
Each of us, whether we hold office or not, shares the responsibility for guiding this most difficult of all societies along the path of self-discipline and self-government.	In your hands, my fellow citizens, more than in mine, will be determined the success or failure of our course.	In your hands, my fellow citizens, more than mine, will rest the final success or failure of our course.

From the Pros, 4 Tips for Passing the "Trip-Easy" Test

❑ Check for words that end in *-sion, -ance, -ment, -ing, -ence,* or *-tion*. Convert those words to trip-easy verbs by dropping the suffix and tweaking the text for fit. For example, "The Company's argument is" becomes "The Company argues that"; "The planners are in violation of" becomes "The planners violate the."

❑ Check for the word *of* and replace with the trip-easy possessive form: "The decision of the council" becomes "The council's decisions."

❑ Check for rambling phrases and replace them with a trip-easy word. For example, "at the time that" becomes "when"; "at this time" becomes "now"; "at that time" becomes "then"; "subsequent to" becomes "after"; "prior to" becomes "before."

❑ Check for word combinations that have a pleasing sound. Bloomingdale's is famous for placing customers' purchases in a beige paper container on which is boldly printed the words "Brown Bag," a much more pleasant sound than if the container was labeled "Brown Sack."

How to Make Your Argument Look Like an Easy Read
Because what appears to be reader-friendly gets read

Take a breather.

Enjoy a cup of coffee.

It's only when you come back that you'll be truly ready for the "Total Look" Test's critical questions.

Look—don't read—at what you have on paper. Replacing periods with semicolons leaves the reader wondering where to pause and reflect. Does your argument look like easy reading? Or something that has to be painstakingly plowed through? Brevity and simplicity (shorter sentences and paragraphs) put your argument within the reader's easy grasp.

How much of your writing is about you? There's a difference between showing what you're all about and egocentric showboating. Chances are better than 50/50 that what you've written is too self-centric. Whatever it is you have to say about your company or yourself is a drag. Later on, you can validate who you are in ways that don't delay or obscure your argument. Check for "I" sentences that are often self-centric: "I feel that a multiplex." "I think that a multiplex." "I believe that a multiplex."

Are your points obvious so that you understand what they mean? Will the reader understand what they mean? Will both you and your reader have the same understanding of what they mean? Reality check: Points don't become obvious just because you say they're obvious. Truly obvious points don't need to be introduced by because-I-say-so words such as *absolutely, it appears that, clearly, definitely, in fact, needless to say, obviously, plainly.*

Now, double-check for bulletproofing...

❐ Are there a "sounds right" core argument and three support- ing points (Chapter 5)?

❐ Will it advance your argument to tell a story (Chapter 4)? Do you use an analogy (Chapter 7)? Do you hone in with surgical strike questions (Chapter 8)? Do you trigger and satisfy the reader's emotional needs (Chapter 9)?

Convincing writing is convincing conversation in print. A winning argument creates trust and throws off "feels right" vibes.

No one will read what you have to say unless you grab and keep their attention.

The three clutter cuts ensure that what you've written is interesting, relevant, and on target.

Move your argument forward in a persuasive progression. Repetition causes readers to become confused. "Detours" throw readers off track.

Trip-easy arguments flow and sweep the reader down the page.

When you're through, look at your argument to make sure it's brief, that it looks like an easy read, and that it has "sounds right" reasoning.

Name Your Ideas

Because the right name is itself a powerful argument

An advertising agency renamed the tinea pedis malady "athlete's foot." Smart move. How likely are you to remember a name like tinea pedis? Could you possibly ever forget "athlete's foot"?

Cosmopolitan's cover could have named its featured recipe "5-minute chocolate mousse." B-O-R-I-N-G. Instead, they called it "5-minute chocolate mousse that will turn your boyfriend into your love slave."

In the early 1990s, the New Jersey Nets was a pro basketball team nobody wanted to see. The Nets lacked charisma, performed poorly, and had no superstars to attract crowds. The allegiance of local fans was across the Hudson River with the New York Knicks. Jon Spoelstra, the Nets president, had a mega marketing problem.

Spoelstra's marketing strategy was not to promote Nets games as great basketball, but as great family entertainment. To jump-start his "family entertainment" campaign, he suggested that the team adopt a name that conveys an image of family entertainment: the New Jersey Swamp Dragons. (The Nets arena is located in the New Jersey Meadowlands, a wetlands area.) The owners rejected Spoelstra's suggestion. That's too bad because the name sounds like a winner, wrote one sports reporter.

Before a shot was fired in the war against Iraq, the Bush administration named the effort Operation Iraqi Freedom. A name that argued to the world that the war had a just cause: helping the Iraqi people. The 1991 Gulf War was named Operation Desert Shield. The name was a "just cause" argument that we were at war to protect the people of Saudi Arabia. Just cause imagery was reflected in the name given to the 2001–2002 war in Afghanistan, Operation Enduring Freedom, and to the 1992–1993 war in Somalia, Operation Restore Hope. The 1989–1990 war in Panama had a name that skipped the imagery and cut right to the chase: Operation Just Cause.

In the anti-multiplex scenario, your argument becomes more forceful when given a name. Two examples: *X-out the multipleX* and *Be a "No Show."*

Craft Tag Lines

Because bite-sized themes are power-uppers

When I say, "You deserve a break today," you think_____.

Car manufacturers know the value of a tag line:

Engineered like no other car in the world.—Mercedes-Benz

The passionate pursuit of perfection.—Lexus

The ultimate driving machine.—BMW

Better engineered. Better made!—Chrysler

And the bicycle people know the value of a tag line: Schwinn realized that it urgently needed to pop a wheelie to put fun back in the bicycle business. The un-Schwinn-like campaign tag: Cars Suck.

There isn't a lot you can say about bottled water. Cascade Clear Mountain Spring Water takes on its big-brand competitors with a wink and let's-not-be-so-serious tag lines: "Water that's not watered down" and "Water just like Grandma used to make."

Tag lines are attention-grabbing, bite-sized themes. In the anti-multiplex scenario, your argument becomes more potent by crafting a tag line: *Multiplex is another way of saying multi-problems.*

How do you know whether the tag line you are considering is a winner? It has to pass the T-shirt test. If it would look and sound good on a T-shirt, then you've got yourself a pretty good tag line.

Orange County, California, wanted the world to know that it was crawling into the black, having emerged from a high-profile bankruptcy. Its pros' advice: a memorable tag line to speed those efforts. After weeks of deliberations, the tag line chosen was "Orange County, The Perfect California." A bad tag line is worse than no tag line at all. Suggestions rejected by the tourism council: "Orange County: So a-peeling" and "Orange you glad you came?"

I know you filled in the tag line blank "McDonalds." McDonald's introduced the tag line in 1971 and used it for four years. It was put back into service in 1981 and 1982. Seems like only yesterday? That's what tag lines are all about. Making points that stick.

Paint Mind Pictures
Because a mind picture is worth a thousand words

Impresarios of influence are artists who paint word pictures to ensure that their argument has clarity and interest.

From a committee chairman's written report: "The suggested proposal, although appearing to have merit, does not present the most viable course of conduct." Legendary journalist H.L. Mencken said it better by painting a word picture: "Just because a rose smells better than cabbage doesn't mean it makes better soup."

And from that same committee chairman's report: "It is important for us to ascertain our customer's true needs and interests rather than accept their remarks at face value." Songwriter Roger Miller said it better by painting this mind picture: "Some people feel the rain. Others just get wet."

In the anti-multiplex scenario, a mind picture can slam home a point. *Just because a guy is fun doesn't mean you want him to move into your home. Multiplexes are fun, but that doesn't mean you want one to move into your neighborhood, down the street.*

Concrete words create mind pictures. Abstract words don't.

I was in the market for new corduroy pants, so I telephoned a local store and spoke to Richard, a salesman.

Bob: Do you have tan cord pants in stock?

Richard: Yes, we just got in a shipment.

Bob: Are they darker or lighter tan? Are they a yellowish tan? Or a reddish-tawny tan?

Richard: More of a brownish-grayish sort of tan. I hate to say this, but I'd call the color "squirrel."

Squirrel was the operative sensory word. My mind was able to picture the brownish-grayish color of our local squirrels and the tan Richard was talking about. And in the what's-happening-out-there department: Macy's features Charter Club terry bath towels and rugs in a color you can visualize because it calls the color "reindeer."

We all remember Katharine Lee Bates 19th-century imagery: "purple mountains majesties" and "amber waves of grain." But if you don't remember the following words from "America the Beautiful," it's because imagery to be effective must be easily understood and easily recalled by others:

> *O beautiful for patriot dream*
>
> *That sees beyond the years*
>
> *Thine alabaster cities gleam,*
>
> *Undimm'd by human tears!*

Do What Noah Did: Bring 'em in Two by Two

Because more than two is too much

"The man is tall and thin." What is the immediate picture you got from this sentence? "The man is short, is bald, wears glasses, and is thin." Did you also get an immediate picture from this sentence? Or did you have to stop for a moment and put the four adjectives together in their proper places?

Plop-Plop, Fizz-Fizz

Because "naturals" add pizzazz to your message

Even as we read silently, we *auralize*—we hear the sounds of words in our mind's ear. Persuasive speakers and writers add excitement by picking words with sounds that fit their message.

Some words have natural sounds: *beep, hush, splash, gobble, clang, yawn, clink, screech, guzzle, squeal.* The musical *Ragtime* advertises "cascading melodies." (Can you almost feel the flow and fall of music?) "It's been years since it was on TV, but no one who saw them will ever forget Alka-Seltzer's "plop-plop, fizz-fizz, oh what a relief it is" commercials.

Take #1: I heard the bell.

Take #2: I heard the bell clang.

Take 1 is lifeless and dull. But what's your take on Take 2?

Use Rhyming Words

Because reason with rhyme is more believable

It's old news. Advertisers use rhyme as a memory aid ("Tough Actin' Tenactin"). What's new is that studies reveal rhyme makes ordinary statements more believable. Consistently, a test group found a statement such as "Woes unite foes" more believable than the statement "Woes unite enemies."

"A profusion of confusion" is what Mr. Blackwell, the famous fashion critic, called the outfit Celine Dion wore to an Oscars ceremony. He could have called it an "abundance of confusion," but that would not have zoomed his message to readers.

"If it doesn't fit, you must acquit" was O.J. Simpson lawyer Johnnie Cochran's rhyming tag line as his soon-to-be-freed client barely squeezed into an incriminating pair of gloves. Do you recall any part of the trial as readily as Cochran's rhyming refrain?

Sizzle and seasoning make your argument more readable, memorable, and convincing.

Name your idea because the right name is itself an argument. Tag lines are bite-sized themes that are your argument's linchpins.

Mind pictures create compelling clarity. Rhyme creates believability.

10 Mix 'n' Match Tricks of the Trade

Because power comes from positioning

Look at magazine and billboard advertising, and notice how marketing masters compel and convince through the placement or repetition of key words, not the repetition of points! When writing, you have the ability to move words and pieces of words around for a mix that powers up your argument with crescendos of emotion, focus, and emphasis.

Trick #1: Repeat words at the beginning.

This is the technique to use when the beginning words or phrases are less important than the ones that follow.

"Who was Dodi Fayed?" was the topic on the *Geraldo Rivera Show*. One of Geraldo's guests suggested that my client, Dodi, may have encouraged the attention of paparazzi on the night he and Princess Diana were killed. A professional spokesperson for the Fayed family persuasively argued otherwise by noting Dodi's very "protective" feelings toward Diana. Here's how he used this technique to power up his impromptu rebuttal: "They were dogged. They were pursued. They were harassed.... He wanted to give her security. He wanted to give her peace. He wanted to give her space."

Trick #2:..at the end...

This is when you want to emphasize the repeated word or phrase.

It was the first game of an American League baseball championship series. A 12-year-old boy stuck out his glove and grabbed a ball that resulted in a game-tying home run for the Yankees. "We were robbed," declared Baltimore's mayor.

"Baseball is a game of breaks. Good calls, bad calls, in-between calls," was New York Mayor Rudolph Giuliani's responsive argument.

Trick #3: or in between.

"SOME WHO QUESTION THE REASON FOR THIS CONFERENCE...LET THEM LISTEN TO THE VOICES OF WOMEN IN THEIR HOMES, NEIGHBORHOODS, AND WORKPLACES. SOME WHO WONDER WHETHER THE LIVES OF WOMEN AND GIRLS MATTER...LET THEM LOOK AT THE WOMEN GATHERED HERE."
—HILLARY CLINTON

Trick #4: Repeat words from the end of one clause at the beginning of the next.

"TO BE PERSUASIVE WE MUST BE BELIEVABLE; TO BE BELIEVABLE WE MUST BE CREDIBLE; TO BE CREDIBLE WE MUST BE TRUTHFUL."
—EDWARD R. MURROW

Trick #5: Repeat prefixes of different words.

"Delegating unclear tasks to an uninspired, unqualified, unorganized committee will be the undoing of our program."

Trick #6: Or repeat the suffix of different words.

"Her idea was scrutinized, analyzed, minimalized, and trivialized, but in the end, it alone made the most sense."

Trick #7: Repeating sounds drive home a point.

Lexus boasts being "passionate in the pursuit of perfection."

Trick #8: Phrases using opposite words are memorable.

"THE COST OF LIVING IS GOING UP AND THE CHANCE OF LIVING IS GOING DOWN."
—FLIP WILSON

Trick #9: A powerful pulsating effect is created by repeating one word over and over.

"NO KITES. NO BALL-PLAYING. NO RUNNING. NO FOOD. NO BEVERAGES. NO THIS. NO THAT."
—SIGN ON THE NEW JERSEY SHORE

Trick #10: Omitting conjunctions gives a staccato effect to your words.

Look what happens when you omit the word *and*:

☐ It was a night to remember. We talked. We danced. We laughed. We cried.

But the repeated use of the conjunction *and* can also be effective:

☐ It was a night to remember. We talked. And we danced. And we laughed. And we cried.

Think back. Which of the 10 tricks do you remember best? Would you have been as readily influenced if the tools of rhyme and repetition had not been called into play?

A bulletproof argument is always in the "basics"—what "feels right" and "sounds right" to the other person.

You can add emotion, feeling, drama, immediacy, or urgency to your argument by tactically repeating and positioning key words and phrases. But overdoing it will be an oversell turnoff.

Don't Get Sucked Into the E-mail Trap

Because what's efficient may not be effective

Star Trek's Mr. Spock transfers information between himself and other Vulcans by touching skulls—mind-meld transfers that are direct and free of emotional content.

So, too, our own Information Age transfers are often direct and free of emotional content. As you become more technologically connected, the less connected you are as a life force—an animate being. Mailboxes are made of pixels instead of aluminum, and texting symbols replace words. High-tech connections lack a hi-touch. In the process, are you abandoning the art of the one-on-one, the people skills that make your arguments compelling?

Always ask yourself: *What's my link-up priority?*

Here's how the persuasion pros see it....

❐ High-tech connecting is about *getting to*. About convenience. Speed. Brevity.

❐ Hi-touch connecting is about *getting through*. About movement. Change.

❐ High-tech is *inanimate*. The cutting edge of soulless connectivity.

❐ Hi-touch is *organic*. It's mystery, magic, and power springing forth from who you are.

❐ High-tech is about *cyber* smarts. About being efficient.

❐ Hi-touch is about *people* smarts. About being effective.

❐ High-tech best deals with "the stuff in the middle." The task-oriented, and the fact-based. The when, where, and how's of your day.

❐ Hi-touch builds trust, resolves conflict, influences outcomes, and helps things go your way.

How will *you* deliver your message? Will you send an e-mail? Fax from an airplane? Drop a letter in the mail? Call for a meeting? Telephone one evening after the tumult of your day has passed?

Each communication medium comes with its own built-in, implicit message.

Want your proposal to deliver the implicit message that "This is it. Take it or leave it"? Then writing may best serve your purpose. Fax and e-mail traffic arrives with the implicit message that its text has special importance and immediacy. Regular "snail mail" conveys the more laid-back message that "There is no rush."

If feedback is more important than the implicit finality of writing, then an interactive medium—a meeting or a phone call—will be your choice. Initiating a live conversation conveys a let's-talk-about-it message. Investing effort in arranging and holding a meeting sends a stronger message that there is a desire to talk things out. If the other guy is skeptical or hostile, you will need a mode that will accommodate more detail and a greater depth of exploration.

According to a former Microsoft employee, James Fallows, in *Atlantic Monthly*, "Microsoft relies as heavily on face-to-face contact as any organization I've ever seen." It's easy to pretend you care. Or that you're concerned. But you can't pretend to be there. Sometimes the necessary alternative to the Internet is the 747.

New technologies can be persuasion facilitators or persuasion obstacles. What are your communication skills? The other side's communication skills? People who are competitive are most effective face-to-face. Cooperative people become bolder using e-mail.

Think about your own experiences with conflict. Maybe it was conflict with your spouse, a boss, an employee, a teacher, a student, a neighbor. If that conflict was ever settled, it was probably because, albeit reluctantly, you met face-to-face to talk out your differences.

As you become more technologically connected, you become less "life-force" connected. In our fast-forward world, we too quickly opt for what's convenient. Winning arguments isn't about what's convenient or efficient. It's about what's effective.

Chapter Summary

It takes time and effort to write a winning argument. But writing may be your only way. Or your best way because of geographic distance, impossible personalities, or complex issues. But with a writing, you're never really sure you'll be read. Whether the reading will be anything more than a fast glance. Or whether you'll even be understood. A writing doesn't provide in-person feedback. On the other hand, a written argument gives the other guy the time and space to reread, absorb, and understand. So, what should you do? For each instance, strategize your alternatives.

Win the War of Words on the Telephone
Because it's becoming harder to travel across town

In this chapter, you'll discover how to get a call through to the person you want to speak to. But you'll also discover that you may not want to make that call. And if a call is made or received, you'll discover the plays to put you at the top of your telephone game.

"I'd like to speak with Jim Smith."

"Let me see if he's here. I'll be just a minute."

(I am wondering, *How can Smith's assistant not know whether he's there, unless there's a secret passage between his office and the parking garage?*)

"I'm sorry, but Mr. Smith isn't here."

"Please have him call me when he returns."

"I would prefer you leave a voice-mail message."

Quick Quiz

Given the choice, will you opt for voice mail or for leaving your message with an assistant?

Dealing With Voice Mail

If you're calling someone for the first time, it may be to your advantage to state your reason for calling on voice mail rather than asking an assistant to deliver it for you. Voice mail is a chance to leave a compelling reason for being called back. What you don't want to do is blurt out your name and number and then hang up. Call it the "Deer in the Headlights" Syndrome—voice-mail messages that sound as if the caller was caught totally off guard. If there's a chance you'll be leaving a recorded message, first jot down what you plan to say.

Leaving Your Message With a Live Person

What about leaving your message with a spouse, assistant, or coworker? Those folks will never convey your thoughts as well as you could in a direct dialogue with the person you called. The message-taker will attempt to relay your message logically, but the person for whom the message is intended may not make his or her decisions based on logic.

If the message-taker conveys your thoughts after several hours or days, he or she probably won't remember everything you wanted said. A voice-mail message may be better than leaving your message with a live person. But read on....

Dealing With a Gatekeeper

Does this sound familiar? How many times a day do you hear a voice-mail response that sounds like this:

"This is Mary Jones. I'm either on another call or not at my desk right now. Please leave a message and I'll call you back as soon as possible."

I punch zero and ask an operator, "Is Mary on another call or is she away from her desk?"

"She is away from her desk."

"Well, is she just down the hall (another way of saying "in the ladies' room")? Or is she out of the office?"

"I'm sorry. Company policy doesn't permit me to tell callers how far our staff members are from their desks."

Be business-like in your dealings with gatekeepers—the people who first take your calls. Speak with confidence and authority, and they'll assume that both you and your message are important. If the gatekeeper thinks you're a jerk, that's what will be reported to the person you're trying to reach. My friend George lost the opportunity to land a big computer hardware contract because he flirted with a prospect's gatekeeper.

How to Sneak Past a Gatekeeper

No one likes being tricked into returning a call. Callers who leave only their first name, or who talk to my assistant as if they were my best friend, make me cast-in-stone resistant. I'd never do business with a cold-caller who tells my assistant that the reason for the call is "private" or "confidential."

To sneak past a gatekeeper, try calling after 5 p.m. Gatekeepers leave work about then and, with luck, your call will ring through to the person with whom you want to speak.

Before you place that telephone call, consider how you'll play the possibilities. Will you opt to hang up rather than leave a voice-mail message? Are you prepared to leave a voice-mail message that is succinct and compelling? Will you be better off leaving your message with an assistant? How will you present yourself to a gatekeeper?

5 Reasons You May Not Want to Make That Call

Because phoning is risky business

You may not want to make or advance your argument in a phone call. Here are five reasons why:

Reason #1: The person you're calling is looking at plastic and cord instead of flesh and blood, so it's much easier to be told no telephonically than in person.

Calls make it all too easy for the other person to verbally walk out of your argument—"I was just running out the door" or "Sorry, but I can't talk right now. I am expecting a call."

Reason #2: It takes patience and effort to be a good telephone listener.

Does your argument require a high degree of concentration? Is it important to explore needs and interests in a lengthy, more fluid dialogue?

Reason #3: A few moments of silence in a meeting is a few moments of silence.

A few moments of silence on the telephone is an eternity. Will you be able to resist the pressure to respond that is inherent in a telephone call? It is always easier to manage sound than silence.

Reason #4: Telephone arguments are briefer and, therefore, more competitive than face-to-face arguments.

Because meetings take time and effort to arrange, by their nature they're chattier and less structured. Will a more personalized strategy better advance your argument? Will a telephone conversation be more or less stressful? Will you be able to construct a telephonic consent zone?

Reason #5: Will the other person be curt if your call interrupts what he or she is doing?

Consider whether alternatives to talking on the phone will better advance your argument.

If you decide to call and the person you want to speak with is on the phone, be sure to put on your PTV.

5 Ways to Have a Persuasive Telephone Voice (PTV)

Because you don't want the personality of a dial tone

On the phone, your voice is you. Whether it's filled with authority, boredom, anticipation, or nervousness, it's the first real clue about you. Here's what you need to know to power up your argument and be at the top of your game:

PTV #1: Avoid a monotone voice.

By letting your voice rise on important words and fall on the not-so-important ones, you will avoid being monotone.

PTV #2: Vary your rhythm to emphasize key points.

Many people believe they are varying their rhythm when in fact they're merely raising or lowering their voice. Rhythm is a matter of pacing—speed.

PTV #3: Visualize your listener.

Instead of staring at the phone or doodling, visualize your listener. With that mental image, you'll project more of your personality.

PTV #4: Enhance your voice by being in motion.

If you talk while keeping your hands, arms, and body still, your voice will reflect the absence of motion. When you wave and point your hands as if your listener were seated across from you, you'll enhance your voice modulation, tempo, and overall drama.

PTV #5: Know your conversation quirks.

Although we're quick to detect conversation quirks in others, we aren't always aware of our own. Are you guilty of *uh-huhs* and other things that drive listeners nuts? Seemingly innocent expressions can irritate a listener when repeated over and over. If you record a few of your telephone conversations, you may discover irritating habits that sap your effectiveness.

11 Tips From the Best of the Best

Because they can make you a telephone pro

Tip #1: Keep it short and simple.

When you use complex sentences and big words, your listener will dwell on what you just said. You'll continue talking, but your listener will be a block behind and you won't have her full attention.

Tip #2: Create mental pictures.

To compensate for not having the benefit of visual aids, create mental pictures that your listener can visualize. One way is to ask "What would happen if…?"

Tip #3: You have the right to remain silent.

Don't feel obliged to fill in conversation lulls. Use lulls to maintain a still center.

Tip #4: Try "conversational harmony."

Someone who speaks softly will feel more comfortable if you speak softly. Someone who speaks loudly will find you a kindred spirit if you match his or her volume. We are most comfortable with the familiar. People who sound and talk like you are seemingly familiar and, therefore, more likely to agree with what you have to say.

Tip #5: Keep your tone of voice in check.

If you sound angry, your listener will become agitated. If you sound calm, you'll exert a soothing influence. An irate person won't stay irate if you don't respond in kind; it's hard to be angry alone.

Tip #6: Be patient.

Repeated interruptions heighten tension. Interrupt only to confirm facts or to clarify a point you missed.

Tip #7: Show you're listening.

Show you are listening by periodically using comments such as "Yes," "I see," and "Go on." To encourage a speaker to keep talking and at the same time confirm you're tracking what he or she is saying, ask questions that begin with phrases such as "Do you mean to say…?" or "Are you saying that…?"

Tip #8: Use the "1-2-3 Technique."

It's easy to jump in too soon, cutting off a speaker with your remarks. By counting 1-2-3 in your head before responding, you leave a pocket of silence for the speaker to add something before you take your turn talking.

Tip #9: Don't feel rushed.

If you can't spare the time to talk, take a moment to acknowledge the call with warmth and sincerity: "It's good to hear from you, Zack!" or "Thanks for returning my call." Then briefly explain why you can't talk and arrange a time to call back.

Tip #10: Be in control.

Sometimes calling back is better than taking an incoming call. When you place a call, control is yours for the taking. You have thought out what you'll say, anticipated questions, insulated yourself from diversions and distractions, and have all the necessary data and information in front of you so nothing is left to guesswork.

Tip #11: Sum it all up.

Conclude your call by reviewing the points that were agreed upon. When you follow up with writing, you reinforce concessions granted and ground gained.

4 Tests to Tell Whether You're Really Getting Through

Because to win you have to be heard

You can't read body language through a telephone receiver, so asking questions is a way to gauge your listener's mood. After you've made four or five statements, ask a question to make sure you're being tracked. Winning arguments isn't about sounding good. Winning is about the other person tracking your ideas and understanding how those ideas fit into your total argument. Here are four tests to see if you're getting through:

❐ Test 1: Is your listener making irrelevant comments?

❐ Test 2: Is your listener asking unnecessary questions?

❐ Test 3: Is your listener asking questions that you already answered?

❐ Test 4: Is your listener saying "I thought you said…" or "You never told me…"?

If the answer to any of these is yes, watch out. You've just veered into an argument cul-de-sac.

Chapter Summary

Think about who will be answering your telephone call. Will it be an assistant? A recording device? Will you want to leave a message? Will you be prepared to leave a message?

There's a difference between being efficient and being effective. There are five tactical reasons why you may be better off not making your argument in a phone call.

If you opt to call, have a PTV and argument-winning manner. The 11 tips from the best-of-the-best give you the winning edge. Use the four tests to tell if you are really getting through to ensure that the other person is listening rather than just hearing your argument.

Win the War of Words With an Audience

Because someday you'll be arguing to an audience of a few or many

In this chapter you'll discover the winning plays for arguing to an audience, plays that are different from those you'd use at less formal meetings.

The words you'll craft for a listener's ears are not the same as the words you'll craft for a reader's eyes. Readers can slow their pace to re-read, to absorb, and to understand—luxuries that listeners don't have.

Write out a rough draft of what you'll say. Even if your talk will be ad-libbed. Unprepared speakers who drift and digress blow their chance to score. Unprepared speakers suffer the *Dan Quayle Syndrome*: a speech with a beginning, a muddle, and an end. "Hawaii is a unique state. It is a small state. It is a state by itself. It is different from other states. Well, all states are different, but it's got a particularly unique situation."

Shuffle your draft's words and sentences around until a "script" emerges. Don't let it be a silent, lonely process. By talking out loud, you'll get the feel of your words and you'll actually hear how they'll sound to others. As you

175

hear your words, you'll discover the emotional side of your argument. It's what energizes your speech. As you shape and sculpt your draft, you'll find yourself expressing ideas, feelings, and emotions that would have never bubbled up had you not talked to yourself out loud.

Don't be surprised if you find yourself stumbling over structured phrases. It's okay to use contractions such as "won't" or "shouldn't" because that's how you speak. Amateurs tend to prepare by writing overly formal talks. Instead of trying to be themselves, they are guided by some abstract notion of what a speaker should be. Overly formal words will only stiffen your natural speech patterns. Your argument should have the flow and feel of a conversation.

Oh–You Beautiful Word

Because most men are droners

"BEFORE I SPEAK, I HAVE SOMETHING IMPORTANT TO SAY."
–GROUCHO MARX

There's no such thing as a persuasive bore. A Canadian judge threw a case out of court because a witness was too boring: "Beyond doubt the dullest witness I've ever had in court...he speaks in a monotonic voice...and uses language so drab and convoluted that even the court reporter cannot stay conscious.... I've had it."

Words are the skin of thoughts. They are abstractions—flat and lifeless. It's your job to bring those abstractions to life. Take the word *oh*. It's just a word. It's how you say *oh* that tells your audience what you mean:

- ❒ Pain: *Oh.* ("My stomach hurts.")
- ❒ A question: *Oh?* ("Is that right?")
- ❒ Excitement: *Oh!* ("Wow!")
- ❒ Boredom: *Oh.* ("How dull.")
- ❒ Disgust: *Oh!* ("Not snow again!")
- ❒ Disbelief: *Oh?* ("Yeah?")
- ❒ Exclamation: *Oh!* ("I forgot to turn off the stove!")
- ❒ Passion: *Oh.* ("I love him/her.")

It's hard to tune out speakers who are genuinely enthusiastic about what they are arguing for. Speakers who gesture well above the podium or move to the side of it. Speakers who use overstated gestures for larger audiences, understated gestures for smaller ones. Speakers who use a leap in pitch, an occasional exaggeration of tone, and changes of tempo and volume to build tension and surprise.

Meet Lee Iacocca
Because he talks plain and simple

Lee Iacocca saved Chrysler Corporation by winning support from Congress and the American people for the biggest corporate bailout in history. Here's how he explained his success: "I've seen a lot of guys who are smarter than I am and a lot who know more about cars. And yet I've lost them in the smoke. Why? Because I'm tough? No.... You've got to know how to talk to them, plain and simple."

The "plain and simple" talk to which he referred was using words to express, not impress. How do you know if a word is pompous? If you wouldn't use it at a cocktail party, chances are it's pompous. Using buzz-words or words only the tech-savvy will understand can also keep you from breaking through.

Quick Quiz

You can't go to a ball game without singing "The Star-Spangled Banner." Without a stadium filled with fans singing with you, run through the words. Have you forgotten a few of them? A New York radio show man-on-the-street poll revealed that not one interviewee knew the words beyond "twilight's last gleaming." Now let me ask you this: Since second grade, you've sung our national anthem's phrase "O'er the ramparts we watched"—but what's a *rampart?*

My high school speech teacher cautioned our class that talks that aren't plain and simple can be fatal. His proof? President William Henry Harrison stood outside in the rain for nearly two hours delivering his inaugural address. He died a month later from pneumonia.

Go Interactive

Because an involved audience is easily won over

People are more easily persuaded when they're actively involved. We quickly forget what we hear, but long remember what we've done. Depending on the size of the audience and your agenda, getting others to share their experiences, opinions, and observations is the way to win.

Interactive speakers with a high degree of eye contact are perceived as being more friendly, natural, self-confident, and sincere. Speakers who make little or no eye contact may come across as cold or evasive. Pauses become powerful when you slowly sweep your eyes across the room.

Tip: In your mind, divide the room into quadrants. When speaking, move from section to section, making eye contact with a handful of selected people in each section.

Be interactive. An audience remembers what they've *done* more than what they've *heard*.

Working With Handouts

Because handouts can be fatal

When arguing to a small or medium-sized audience, you can distribute handouts, although you may not want to distribute handouts until long before or long after you're done speaking. Ask any teacher. Chances are he or she knows the name Lee Canter. Lee is America's number-one educator. His textbooks and programs teach teachers how to teach.

A good part of law is waiting. As Lee and I watched a room full of lawyers argue their cases, it happened over and over again. A lawyer would come forward; the judge would then pick up and read that lawyer's brief; and as the judge read, the lawyer would verbally argue his or her position. Lee was shocked and whispered to me, "These lawyers don't know what every good teacher knows about getting through. You don't talk to people while they're reading. When you do, neither your written nor your spoken words will be fully absorbed nor remembered."

Back in the neighborhood: Hand out maps of the multiplex's anticipated traffic flow patterns in and through the neighborhood after you speak and answer questions. Make your argument more interactive.

Distribute handouts long before or after you speak. Handouts that are read while you're talking only detract from what you're saying.

Pros Use Props

Because complicated ideas call for simple demonstrations

Moses came down from the mountain bearing clay tablets. Would the impact have been the same if he simply announced without tablets, "Ten things were told to me by God. I'm here to tell you what they are."

The nation was about to enter World War II. A single limp noodle on a plate was the prop General George Patton used to impress upon his junior officers what he expected of them. With his officers standing around a large table, the general tried pushing the noodle forward with his fingers. The noodle only squiggled and twisted. Patton then snatched up one end of the noodle and swept it across the plate. In no uncertain terms he made his point: "Gentlemen, you don't push...you lead!"

Use a prop such as a videotape showing cars fighting to get into a multiplex parking lot and the congestion caused by the moviegoers leaving.

I found a great prop in a T-shirt shop. To humorously drive home the point that sometimes we overlook the obvious, I held up a shirt that asked the burning question, "Why isn't there mouse-flavored cat food?"

4 Ways to Get Your Butterflies to Fly in Formation

Because you don't have to be a nervous wreck

Arguing to an audience isn't a life-or-death situation—although a dry throat, sweaty palms, and a pounding heart may make it feel that way. Here are four relaxers that are guaranteed to keep you from being a total nervous wreck:

❑ **Relaxer #1:** When your talk is well in mind, time yourself. Then rehearse again, but this time take a third longer. A slower pace will slow your breathing and lessen your jitters.

❑ **Relaxer #2:** World-class athletes know the importance of visualization when preparing for an event. Visualizing the execution of a perfect play gives them confidence. As you prepare to argue imagine the situation down to the last detail—how you will stand, what you will say, where you will look, how the room and the audience will appear—and let yourself experience the anxiety. The fear won't disappear, but you'll become familiar with it.

❑ **Relaxer #3:** Get to know your audience. Arrive early to mingle with the folks who will be hearing you. Introduce yourself to as many new faces as possible. That way you won't be addressing a room full of strangers.

Take a tip from major league ball players who, one-on-one, will chat before a game about odds and ends or about themselves. Chit-chat before a talk relieves tension and a nervous tummy.

❑ **Relaxer #4:** Wait to talk for five or 10 seconds after arriving at the spot where you'll be speaking. Just by being silent—you need do nothing more—you will seize control of time and space as your audience bonds together in collective anticipation of what you'll be saying.

3 Cures for the Common Speech

Because a speech and a bowl of popcorn have something in common

Popcorn without salt and butter is filling. It has nutritional value. But it's also boring and not much fun to eat. Unseasoned speeches faithfully convey information. They're boring and make for hard listening. So here's the seasoning: three cures for the common speech.

Cure #1: Verbally highlight your main points.

Layer your three portable points between simple, outside-the-box grabbers. Your audience will stay tuned in, and the portable points you need to get across will stand out.

Here are some fun and easy ways to step outside the box:

- ❐ **Songs:** "We were global when global wasn't cool," declared the president of Cola-Cola (the actual lyrics of the Barbara Mandrell classic are "I was country when country wasn't cool").

- ❐ **Bits and pieces:** Scan newspapers and magazines for items that can spice up your argument. When talking about where ideas come from, I like to tell how UCLA researchers, hoping to design a better football helmet, studied why woodpeckers don't get headaches—a neat "aside" from the pages of *FYI*.

- ❐ **Movies:** The current hits always have memorable lines. From years past: "Make my day." "May the force be with you." "Show me the money." "Life is like a box of chocolates."

Cure #2: Your subject may be mundane, but you can't be.

Senator Sam Ervin Jr. was best-known for leading the investigation of the Watergate scandal. When he was 85, he reminded us that humor can clarify the obscure. Deflate the pompous. Chastise the arrogant. And simplify the complex. The humor that Sam Ervin was talking about was humor that percolates out of the context of your talk and includes the audience in the fun.

A parrot, a lawyer, and a jockey walk into this bar....

Don't open with a canned joke. Not even if it's funny. Unless you're a gifted story-teller, opening with a joke is risky business. If you don't get a laugh, you're standing there with egg on your face. But if you still feel you have to tell that opening joke....

President Jimmy Carter wasn't much at telling funny stories. On a visit to Japan, he told a joke that had his audience laughing and clapping. Carter was so pleased with the response that he later asked his translator how he had interpreted the story for the audience. "I told them you had just told a joke, so they should laugh," the translator confessed.

If you tell a joke and it's greeted with silence, it's not only embarrassing, but you'll probably be thrown off your stride. But if you tell the audience, "I heard a funny story the other day...," your audience will know something humorous is coming up and will hopefully self-program itself to laugh.

Cure #3: Use a great quote.

Here's the reality. Not all quotes are quotable. Not all quotes are great. And using quotes outside your own area of competence may make you sound pretentious and phony.

When Pope John Paul arrived at the Miami airport, the pontiff's half-smile gave President Reagan's game away. Regan, in welcoming the Pope, quoted Thomas Aquinas. The Pope smiled, knowing that Reagan hadn't really read Aquinas. And everyone else who saw Reagan on the evening news knew that the President wasn't familiar with Thomas Aquinas. The point: Quotes can't be from outside your area of competence. If they are, you'll only look foolish.

Using any quote that is longer than 30 or so words is probably a mistake. Keep your argument from being a snooze-fest by layering your core argument's points between grabbers. By using humor that isn't canned or contrived. Use humor that bubbles up and flows from the context of your talk. And use quotes that are brief, relevant, and entertaining. "There's no thief like a bad book." This short and entertaining Italian proverb reminds us that a bad book steals our time and gives nothing back in return.

Visual Aids Are Not Always the Stuff of Winning Arguments

Because data overload is a turnoff

Visual aids and props can enhance the clarity and power of your argument. The more complex your argument, the more it helps to translate your points into a chart, graph, or other visual form. But boring numbers and text outlines don't become interesting just because they're projected on a screen or dolled up with computer graphics.

Put yourself in your audience's shoes. Most of us really don't want to read and absorb multiple concepts and long-winded factual scenarios.

Be honest. When was the last time you were wowed by anybody's graphics? Cool it on data overload. Keep visual aids to a bare-bones minimum, and don't read what's on the screen if your audience is at all literate. Instead, say something new. Here are two visual *never evers*:

1. *Never ever* disconnect from your audience by talking to the words on a screen or flip chart instead of the people in front of you.

2. *Never ever* rely on visual aids to guide you through your speech. A visual aid is an aid—something to enrich or make your talk more vivid. Aids that overpower your oral presentation are counterproductive.

5 Tips to Tilt the Playing Field
Because a talk is like a love affair

Tip #1: It's best to be the leadoff batter.

If you aren't the only speaker, try to lead off. True, by presenting your argument first, the speakers who follow will be able to attack your argument. And yes, you'll be at a disadvantage not knowing what those later in the lineup will say. You, however, will have the first crack at winning over your audience—and that alone makes it worthwhile to lead off. If you can't go first, then position yourself to go last.

Tip #2: Tell the person who will introduce you to just cool it.

It's their nature. Introducers always over-embellish. The person who introduces you will tell the crowd how wonderful you are. Your ability to convince is sapped because the crowd will be thinking, *Can anybody really be all that good? She has a lot to prove before I'm convinced.* The surest way to prevent introducer over-hype is for you to write out what you want the introducer to say.

If your credentials are weak, your ability to persuade will be lessened because of who you aren't. But if you speak without an embellished introduction and your audience likes what you have to say, finding out later that your credentials are on the skimpy side won't have much of a negative impact.

Tip #3: Try not to use that old "I'm glad to be here" stuff.

Open with a statement or question that reaches out, sets the theme of your argument, and grabs the audience. After you deliver a captivating introduction you can, if you want, express your thanks.

Winston Churchill said, "I never say 'it gives me great pleasure' to speak to any audience because there are only a few activities from which I derive intense pleasure, and speaking is not one of them." It was a precept Churchill only violated once. At the Other Club, an informal group organized to discuss ideas and politics, and extemporaneous talks were a traditional rite. From a hat, a club member's name was drawn. From another hat, a topic was drawn. The name drawn was Churchill and the topic drawn was sex. Churchill rose and, holding up the topic card, began, "It gives me great pleasure…." He then sat down.

Tip #4: Remember: A talk is like a love affair.

A friend of mine who is a persuasive speaker and a man-about-town kinda guy insists speeches are like love affairs. They're easy to start, but bringing them to an end requires considerable skill.

To give your argument a well-packaged feel, connect your conclusion to your introduction. Here are two good ways you can do this and at the same time keep your audience locked in: Start with a riddle that you answer in your conclusion, or open with a suspenseful story that you finish as part of your closing. Power up your closing by briefly retelling your main points in a fresh and memorable way, followed by your call for action.

You should be so familiar with your close that you can close without looking away from your audience.

Tip #5: Stay aloft when winging it.

If you're called on to speak unexpectedly, the normal adrenaline rush response is to think about what you'll say to open. Instead, devote whatever time you have to how you are going to close. It's the finish that your audience takes home.

If you know there's a possibility you'll be asked to "say a few words," prepare some *elevator speeches* in advance. These are mini-talks keyed to your three main points. You should be able to start and finish an elevator speech in the two or three minutes it takes for an elevator ride in an average office building.

When winging it, your natural reaction will be to throw out nonstop, off-the-cuff remarks to keep from pausing. But pauses are good. They let you think about where you're going and what you want to say next.

To Memorize or Not to Memorize?

Because you have alternatives

He's the man they called "The Great Communicator." (We won't deny him this well-deserved title because of that blunder at the Miami airport.) One of Ronald Reagan's super-secrets was to memorize only the critical segments of his talk. Reagan's delivery appeared informal because the cement—what he said between his memorized segments—didn't have a committed-to-memory sound or feel.

Lindsey Graham, Republican senator from South Carolina, spoke at Bill Clinton's impeachment proceedings. Unlike the 12 lawyers who preceded him, Graham didn't read from a prepared text. He had notes, but he seldom referred to them. Instead, he kept his eyes on his listeners. All the senators seemed awake at the same time. For the first time in three days, they stopped squirming and scribbling. Graham's plain-spoken style and use of understandable metaphors had captured their attention.

If you must read, then make your words conversational. You want to be a persuasive speaker, not just a good reader. But consider this: A guaranteed-to-work alternative to reading or memorizing is to type out just the key words and phrases of your argument using a good-sized font and bold letters. Have no more than a few words or phrases on any line. The written phrases or parts of phrases should be so brief that you can *scan* and *scoop them up* instantaneously. Words that connect phrases are clutter, so leave them out. Instead, type in ellipses (…) to separate phrases.

Because it's easy to lose your sense of time, most amateurs will rush through their talk. Type in slash marks (////) to remind yourself to pause. Each slash can represent a one-second pause. You will have both long (/////////) and short pauses (//). Put in lots of pauses. Pauses signal your audience to think about what you just said—that you've stopped talking so they can absorb.

With everything in place, you're now able to quickly look down, scoop up a word or phrase, then look at someone in the audience and speak. And then again quickly look down, scoop up another word or phrase, look at someone else in the audience, and speak.

A lecture circuit pro uses only the top half of each page so he doesn't have to look down. To avoid the flying-page syndrome, he never staples pages together. When he finishes a page, he just slides it to the side. He boldly numbers each page in the upper right-hand corner. If his pages get out of order, he is ably prepared to quickly remedy the situation.

Here's the opening of Lincoln's Gettysburg Address:

Four score and seven years ago, our fathers brought forth

on this continent, a new nation, conceived in Liberty, and

dedicated to the proposition that all men are created equal.

What did Abraham Lincoln actually say when he delivered the Gettysburg Address? No one knows because nobody wrote down Lincoln's thoughts word for word. The opening lines you just read were from a version of his address jotted down later. We do know that Lincoln stood at Gettysburg holding—but not reading—his talk.

If Lincoln had notes, perhaps they would have looked like this:

Four Score...7...//

Our fathers...continent...new nation.///

Conceived...Liberty//

And dedicated...equal////

If you practice, the missing words will be there for you when you speak. So what if your talk isn't letter-perfect? Arguments aren't won with antiseptic readings. They are won by what is hi-touch and has a heart-driven color and feel.

A brochure for handwoven carpets boasts the carpets' imperfections in color and symmetry of design. It points out how imperfections are inherent in a product crafted entirely by hand. How imperfections are desired more than "the uniformity of color, design, and dimensions" that you get with a machine-made carpet. Link up by letting your personality—imperfections and all—come through in your spoken argument.

Notes are a safety net—but only a net. Being a great reader doesn't win arguments. Being a conversational speaker does. Content is a totality. You're always both: your argument's message and its messenger.

Emergency Moves

Because there are three ways to jump-start a dead-in-the-water talk

People generally speak at a rate of 120 to 150 words per minute (WPM). Our brains can process 500 WPM—plenty of time left over for mental fidgeting. When a speaker is droning on, monotonic, and wordy, his or her audience will lapse into a fake listening mode rather than struggling to stay tuned.

Most speakers are so busy talking that they miss the telltale signs that they're losing their audience. The following three red-flag warnings signal that you're in trouble:

1. People are flipping ahead in their handouts.

2. People are looking around. An interested audience will look directly at you unless they're busy taking notes.

3. The buzz level rises. As listeners become restless, they will start to whisper to those around them.

And here's the antidote…. Three tricks to jump-start your talk and reenergize your audience are:

Jump-Start #1: Pull something out of left field.

A speaker referred to "an idea so big it was Jurassic." A luncheon speaker whose topic was "What to Do When the Internal Revenue Service Is in Hot Pursuit" asked his audience the heads-up-and-take-notice question: "Are you having sex with the IRS?" Prepare two or three relevant zingers ahead of time for use when needed.

Jump-Start #2: Toss in a pregnant pause before a key idea.

With a seven- to 10-second pause, listeners will look at you because they're curious what you'll say next.

Jump-Start #3: Ask questions.

Questions do more than liven things up. Their answers tell you how it's going and what your audience wants to learn down the road. For example: "What are some of the things you would like to know?" or "Where do you stand on this?"

Q&A Tips

Because at the end, audiences always ask questions

Taking questions and answers at the end of your talk will detract from your argument's close and call for action. Consider taking questions during your presentation or later informally. But if a Q&A session is required....

Tip #1: Relax.

If you know your subject matter well, you'll be able to answer most questions easily. You'll be more relaxed if you think of a question as an indication of interest rather than a challenge.

Tip #2: Collect your thoughts.

If a question catches you off guard, take time to collect your thoughts by repeating it. If you don't know the answer to a question, respond, "That's a terrific question! Let's throw that one open for discussion. Who wants to comment on that?"

Tip #3: Use humor.

Using humor to respond to a difficult question is risky. You never want to look like you're making fun of the questioner or ignoring the other person's concerns. A humorous acknowledgment should always be followed by a serious explanation.

Tip #4: Don't drag on.

Limit all of your answers to two minutes maximum. If a questioner wants more details, offer to meet with him or her one-on-one when your talk is finished.

Tip #5: End on a high note.

Winding up your Q&A session by calling for "one last question" can backfire if that question turns out to be dull, negative, or one you don't know how to answer. Instead, say, "We have time for just a few more questions," then end your argument on a high note—after the next good question.

Thou Shall Be Cool
Because you may encounter a heckler

Hecklers need to be heard. That need may be a more important need than extracting an answer from you.

Acknowledge your heckler's question, but keep your eyes away from him or her. When you lock eyes with a heckler, you're in danger of losing the rest of your audience. Portray the heckler as someone who is trying to build a barrier between you and your audience by reminding the audience of why you're there: "I can address that issue a little later on, but for now I'm going to stick to the agenda and cover the points everyone has come to hear." But if you do decide to respond, wait and respond when the time is right for you.

4 Plays to Finesse Hostile Questions
Because you can't hatch chicks from fried eggs

Recall the empowering secrets of a still center.

Defense Play #1: Finesse loaded questions.

Speak in a firm, calm, controlled voice: "I'm glad you asked that question. Others who once disagreed with me expressed that very same concern" or "At one time I felt differently, just as you do now. But after having seen with my own eyes what's happening on the streets where there are multiplexes, I now look at things differently. Let me tell you why...."

It's a *feel, felt, found* approach: "I understand how you feel. Many others once felt just as you do. They found, however, that...."

Finesse a loaded question by rephrasing it in neutral terms before trying to answer it:

Question: Why did your company stop sponsoring college scholarships?

Answer: I have been asked why our company had to make such a hard choice.

Defense Play #2: Focus on your bottom line.

There is no rule that you have to respond to every point raised. You should, however, acknowledge what's been asked. Every time you answer a question, it's an opportunity to make a point—even though that point isn't directly related to the question. The *boomerang tactic* loops a question back to your core argument: "I understand what you've said. The bottom line issue that must be addressed is...."

Defense Play #3: Anticipate.

Second-guess what will be asked by coming up with the questions you'd pose if you were on the other end of the stick. Then, come armed with an arsenal of your best bits—punchy one-liners, imaginative analogies, quick-to-grasp statistics, arm-twisting facts. You'll never be on the spot when you've anticipated the questions and have an arsenal of answers.

Defense Play #4: Steer clear of hostility.

It's your tone of voice that empowers you to control a hostile confrontation. Rather than meeting hostility with hostility, modulate your voice and tone so your response is slow, deliberated, and soft-spoken.

If a hostile questioner persists, don't say "We're running out of time" or "I think this is getting too involved." Instead, have a positive comeback: "That's an interesting point. Let's discuss it further during the break." Then quickly break eye contact and search the room for the next inquiry.

Press Conference Reporter: Can you name one president that has told more lies?

Joe Lockhart, Clinton White House Spokesman: I don't think I'm going to take that question.

Chapter Summary

When providing your audience with a written argument, you're never sure whether you've broken through. With a talk, you'll get immediate feedback. But playing out your argument in a talk has its slippery slopes. Be prepared to do it right or don't do it at all.

Win the War of Words at a Meeting
Because PTAs, neighborhoods, and offices love meetings

Arguing at a meeting requires having what the pros call a "Meeting Mentality."

In this chapter you'll discover the tactics and strategies of a Meeting Mentality. Plays that are different from those you would use in a speaker/audience setting (see Chapter 14).

Quick Quiz

You are a PTA parent, one of a group of parents and teachers who will be meeting to discuss how the school's share of state lottery monies should be allocated. You know that some will argue for buying more computers. Some will be arguing to expand sports programs. Others will be arguing for expanding cultural enrichment activities, such as museum field trips and new instruments for the school orchestra. You will be arguing for after-school tutoring programs for kids who would otherwise fall hopelessly behind in their studies.

How and when during the meeting should you argue?

The meeting will be held in the school library, where there is a large rectangular table. Where should you sit?

Should you argue early or later in the meeting?

What should you say if another parent asks, "Are you arguing for a tutoring program because your own child would benefit?" (That isn't why you're supporting the program, but it's true you have a child who would benefit.)

7 At-the-Meeting Tactics You Must Know

Because your argument starts before the meeting begins

Tactic #1: The more people you know at the meeting, the more confident you will be when you make your argument.

Arrive early and get to know the others who will be there. Now is the time to test the waters by approaching key decision-makers one-on-one to solicit their support.

Tactic #2: People who talk more are perceived as leaders.

Most people who have a point of view will either not speak up or will simply play it by ear. Your argument will be more forceful than theirs if you're prepared to support it and know how you'll tackle opposing points of view.

Tactic #3: People who contribute early are more likely to have the most influence.

Join the discussion early on. Keep your remarks short, simple, and direct. Use limited visual aids to illustrate main points. People remember more of what they see than of what they hear. Remember: You're less likely to be interrupted if you don't have to rummage through your notes looking for back-up information.

Tactic #4: Your points will be better understood if you ask questions.

Questions cause people to think. A good rule of thumb: Talk no more than a minute or so without asking a question. Questions can be those that you wait for the group to answer or those you answer yourself.

Tactic #5: Your argument—no matter how great it is—is bound to meet resistance.

Don't roll your eyes as if your opposer is the most stupid person on earth. No, not even if it's true. Make it easy for opposers to gracefully backpedal by sharing credit for ideas that stem from your discussion. Check out the Defense Plays in Chapter 14. They'll guide you through the wilderness and keep you on high ground.

Make eye contact. Looking down is a sign of weakness. By looking the other fellow in the eye, he'll know you're listening. It's a normal urge to race to your own defense. But keep a *still center* and resist by pausing, gathering your thoughts, and discussing them calmly. To appear less aggressive, say, "Let me play devil's advocate for a minute," then calmly state your argument.

Tactic #6: Interrupting to correct an inaccuracy or make your argument will only make things worse.

Interruptions breed more interruptions. Winston Churchill once admonished his opposer: "Don't interrupt while I'm interrupting!" Wait until he's done talking and put him on the defensive, by asking "What would you have done?" or "What's your positive suggestion?" Use *surgical strike questions* that point to solutions. Don't get bogged down with details. Instead, focus on the big picture. ("Let's stop a second and remember that the whole point of our meeting is to....")

Tactic #7: Control is lost when you wait for others to take the first shot.

Be in control of your own message. Beat others to the punch by calling out the negatives and dealing with them, rather than waiting for others to call them out. Avoid becoming defensive. This is how a CEO reported on a bad year to a meeting of shareholders:

"Clearly, we had some very fundamental problems. Our cost of goods was escalating, placing us ever closer to the bottom tier of companies in our peer group. Our return on investment was slipping. Cash flow targets weren't being met. Inventories were rising. The need to act was evident, and we did.... We are now very confident about the future."

Arrive early and solicit pre-meeting support. Make your argument early in the meeting. Ask questions that get others to think about what you've said. Don't interrupt others who have opposing points of view because they will only interrupt back.

10 Tactics for Both Arguing at and Chairing the Meeting

Because you have the power to choreograph a win

Tactic #1: Make sure the meeting is necessary.

Calling an unnecessary meeting will make you look ineffective. Ask yourself: *Is a meeting really necessary? Can I avoid cutting into everybody's busy day by making a few telephone calls or writing a memo? Which alternative will best advance my argument?*

Tactic #2: Limit the number of attendees.

The more people in attendance, the harder it will be to get what you're arguing for. If you want fewer people in attendance, narrow the meeting's focus and keep your objectives specific.

Tactic #3: Build a Consent Zone.

Set the tone of the meeting by making good news announcements or sharing a personal anecdote that will tie into why you called the meeting.

If the attendees are strangers to each other, let everyone introduce themselves. Go beyond just asking each person his or her name and what he or she does by posing a question as each person is introduced. The question should be keyed to the purpose of the meeting ("What is one thing you'd like to learn by being here?"). A great way to get everyone to focus on how they can make the meeting productive is to have attendees introduce themselves not by their titles, but by explaining what they bring to the meeting's "team effort."

Create a Consent Zone meeting environment. A lunch or dinner meeting may not best advance your argument. Let others say their piece. Vote early and often.

Tactic #4: Know the importance of setting.

Setting is a critical component of the persuasion progression. If you want to be clearly in control, sit at the head of a rectangular table or stand facing the group. If you want to try to encourage attendees to interact, choose a seat at or close to the middle of the table.

You can appear democratic and still maintain your position of leadership if you take the end seat on one side of the table and seat no one at the head or the foot.

To reduce open confrontation, reduce eye contact by seating your opponents on the same side of a rectangular table a few seats away from you. On the other hand, by arranging the seating in a circle, everyone will be able to see everyone easily and will feel more connected.

Tactic #5: Keep it short and to the point.

The attention span of the average person in a meeting plummets after an hour. Unless you want to establish a social (as well as a business) relationship with attendees, don't call a lunch or dinner meeting. Instead, devote all of your productive time to accomplish your specific goals.

Your meeting will run quickly if it is scheduled for 11 a.m. or 4 p.m. These times are an hour before lunch and quitting time, and participants will be more likely to keep their input short and to the point.

Tactic #6: Know your goals.

The most productive meetings are the ones where you clearly set out your argument's goals and refer to them often. Distribute handouts well before the meeting begins. Meetings go faster when attendees already have background information on agenda items.

Tactic #7: Keep on track.

To keep the meeting moving, limit discussions to one agenda item at a time. When discussions veer off track, remind the group that "This is the issue we're discussing...."

If the meeting is in a go-nowhere-mode (you'll know because everyone will be repeating themselves) restate the issue in contention and summarize any ground that has been covered. If the group still can't agree, or if it appears a decision would be adverse to you, table the issue.

Tactic #8: State objections early.

Others are more likely to support an unpopular position if they've a chance to say their piece. You can force a decision, but you can't force commitment. Hostility is defused when participants sound their objections early on. ("Let's take some time to get objections out in the open.") Divide big problems into smaller, more manageable ones. Taking a short break will sever old conversations and allow you to start new ones.

Tactic #9: Show you're listening.

Validate that you've heard the other guy by writing what he said on your notepad or on a flip chart or board.

Tactic #10: Vote early and often.

More will be accomplished if you call for votes early and often. It's a waste of time and energy to permit an in-depth analysis of every point. When it appears there is consensus on one of your points, vote on that item and move on to the next point.

Chapter Summary

Put a winning move into play before the meeting even begins. If you're chairing the meeting, choreograph an outcome that will be to your liking.

Heavy Metal Moves
Because they shape how others will act and react

Lawyers at an American Bar Association Dispute Resolution Conference "had to look twice when they saw rock stars from the band KISS."

It turned out they were the conference faculty.

Why KISS? "To make a serious point": When resolving conflict, sometimes you'll need "skills from the dark side". Skills known as "Heavy Metal". The faculty discussed "taboo subjects such as manipulation, intimidation."[1]

Here are three pass-on-from-generation-unto-generation truths:

☐ Truth #1: Escalating the conflict only prolongs the conflict.

☐ Truth #2: Conflict follows a path. Emotional responses gradually regress from a mature to an immature level.

☐ Truth #3: As conflict escalates, people take a stand rather than trying to understand.

Add it up: Truth 1 + Truth 2 +Truth 3 = Winning may depend on busting through now—not later.

Heavy Metal Moves throw the other guy off balance by creating feelings of self-doubt, negatively charging expectations, creating mental fatigue, and gnawing away at how he perceives his power. When he's physically or psychologically uncomfortable, a concession or two is a small price to pay to cut discussions short and be on his way.

Heavy Metal Moves aren't about being a bad-ass or a hard-ass. But "sometimes you need to be a bully to get what deserve," noted *AARP* magazine.[2]

No one move is so universal that it'll work in every situation. Be intuitive. Pick and choose. Don't overkill. Too many is too much.

Most Heavy Metal Moves are no stronger than your own credibility. The ability to win increases when you substantiate critical facts and the source of those facts.

Heavy Metal Moves can't appear calculating or manipulative. They have to come across as unplanned and spontaneous.

Technique is the art of application. The same paint can be applied with a fine brush or an industrial roller. It depends on when and what you want to accomplish. A "fine brush" is about finessing your desired outcome. An"industrial roller" is about laying it on thick—going Heavy Metal. Same paint. Two application styles. Discriminate wisely.

Tactic #1: Convert molehills into mountains.

The Department of Defense is notorious for overpaying for basic supplies. But somehow it doesn't seem like overpaying when the Department's manual converted molehills into mountains by referring to a steel nut as a "hexiform rotatable surface compression unit," and a tent as a "frame-supported tension structure."

Create bogus issues. Claim what's secretly unimportant is of great importance. If you're pressed for an explanation say, "for a lot of reasons," or "it's personal," or "it's just something that I can't concede." The key is not to get into specifics that can be argued.

Inflate the value of your throwaway points. Everything has a price. An exchange value: "Maybe if my arm is twisted, I'd consider giving in on that point. But only under the right circumstances." What are those circumstances? "Well, I might agree if you're willing to...."

Because of a kitchen fire, the Jones family needs new kitchen cabinets in time for the Smith family annual Thanksgiving dinner. Jones asks you, a kitchen contractor, if the work could be completed in two weeks. Business is slow and that's something you can easily and gladly do. *No problem* would normally be your answer. But that would be tossing out a *throwaway point.* A point that you can inflate to *primary point* status: *"If you want the cabinets in just two weeks, there'll have to be a 15% rush fee."* The tactic is to create added exchange value. For the Jones's contractor, the new value offered is acceleration of the delivery date. Arguing has an underlying bargaining component (bargaining itself is a form of argument) and this is a bargaining tactic. You converted a molehill to a mountain and made 15 percent more in the process.

Sometimes price has the power build to a mountain out of a molehill....

The *Journal of the American Medical Association* reported "that researchers found that people given identical pills got greater pain relief from they one they were told cost $2.50 than from the one supposedly costing ten cents."[3]

We believe that a pair of $200 designer jeans will fit better and be made better than a pair from Wal-Mart. Why do we believe it? Because they cost $200. So what if a world away, they're made in the same factory by the same factory workers?

Tactic #2: Be a power sapper.

Feeling that you have power is power. By managing how the other guy feels about himself, by sapping his feeling of power, you manage how effectively he'll argue against you.

Power is sapped, expectations are manipulated, and nerves are rattled when the other person keeps rescheduling your appointment. And when you do finally show up, she keeps you waiting in the reception room. Nobody offers you a cup of coffee. Outdated reception room magazines go better with a cup of coffee. She finally meets with you. Or, as they say at the Vatican, "grants you an audience."

Staff members continuously pop in and out of her office with messages. And all the while, "Her Majesty" makes nitpicky comments about your company and its services. And as far as your proposal? You're not sure. But it sure seems as if she couldn't care less.

None too soon for you, she stands up at her desk, a sign your meeting is over. And yes, she'll look your proposal over. The last thing you hear as you're escorted to the door are some very nice words about your competition.

You can chalk it all up to her having a really bad day. Or you can chalk it up to having been skillfully manipulated by a pro. If you weren't ready to make concessions before, you are now.

Tactic #3: Manipulate expectations.

People are guided by their expectations. Expectations influence how we process information and how we make decisions.

At MIT there was an experiment with MBA students. Thinking they were part of a school cafeteria survey, the students sampled free coffee. They were then asked questions about the coffee. How much did you like the brew? What's the top price you'd pay for a cup of that brew?

Some students tried the coffee when it was poured from beautiful containers sitting on attractive trays. Container labels were nicely printed. Small silver spoons sat on the tray.

For others, the coffee was served in Styrofoam cups cut shorter by hand. The label on those cups was printed with a felt-tip pen.

The experiment revealed that when the coffee service was upscale, the coffee tasted upscale. The service ambience impacted expectations.

An accountant I met at a dinner party told me about his "sure fire" marketing plan. He was going to raise his hourly rates by 30 percent. He wanted potential clients to believe he was more tax-planning-savvy than his less expensive competitors.

Tactic# 4: Be a pile driver.

"IF YOU HAVE AN IMPORTANT POINT TO MAKE, DON'T TRY TO BE SUBTLE OR CLEVER. USE A PILE DRIVER. HIT THE POINT ONCE. THEN COME BACK AND HIT IT AGAIN. THEN A THIRD TIME—A TREMENDOUS WHACK."
—WINSTON CHURCHILL

A pile driver is one who hits or attacks something powerfully. A pile driver voice and attitude can be effectively intimidating. Heads up: Do you have a good solid argument? If so, amplification that goes beyond pile driving will detract from the points you want to get across. There's the force of logic. And then there's the logic of force. Consider how you'll best play the pile driver game.

Tactic #5: Go theatrical.

Be mad. Be Angry. Be righteously indignant. If need be, throw a temper tantrum into the mix. Theatrics may well prompt concessions, an apology, an act of appeasement. Will the other side pretend they don't care that you've gone ballistic? Or will they concede just to be done with your off-the-wall theatrics?

Tip: If you expect the other person is going to be theatrical and loud, then meet at a quiet restaurant. No one wants to embarrass themselves in a room filled with diners.

Tactic #6: Make 'em feel desperate.

It's a tactic that insurance adjusters and tax collectors put into play.

The claims adjuster with whom I'd been negotiating with for several weeks told me, "Our negotiations have been going on way too long." His department manager has advised him that "a senior adjuster will be taking over the claim file." He then warned me in a whispered voice, "That senior adjuster has a reputation for being very, very, very difficult."

I was on notice: Unless I accepted the adjuster's previously rejected settlement offer, I'd be forced to deal with Mr. Super Difficult. I was at risk of losing the ground I had gained. Defensive tip: Don't become desperate just because you are being told to become desperate.

Tactic #7: Make them invest in you.

Make the other guy invest time, energy, or money in you, maybe by gathering relevant information as to your needs, preparing a proposal, drafting bid plans, or spending time explaining options and alternatives. The greater his investment in you, the greater his propensity to grant concessions. It makes good business sense. Granting concessions and resolving differences is better than losing his investment altogether.

Tactic #8: Auction action

On cruises, I enjoy watching art auctioneers skillfully agitate bidders into a competitive frenzy. Passengers with no intent of buying are entertained by these at-sea reality shows. When the hammer falls, the price paid may be far more than what would've been paid for the same item in a hometown gallery.

When you're working (or appear to be working) with several competitors at the same time, you create an auction climate. The other fellow's need to win the race may be fueled more by his emotion than by logic.

When emotions are summoned into play, he'll grant irrational concessions. Concessions are the price he pays to beat the competition.

Tactic #9: Bluff.

You're in an argument. The other fellow has a full-of-himself attitude, acting as if he were *the* authority. Now is the time to level the playing field by asking questions that can't be answered: "Wasn't there a CNN program that was very critical of that position? Knowing you like to be informed, I doubt you would've missed it."

Okay, you were just bluffing. But then, you'll find bluffing at the heart of virtually every competitive activity.

Tactic #10: Build a wall-of-flesh.

Why argue one-on-one when you can argue three- or four-on-one? Surround an adversary with a wall-of-flesh. If you're going to meet to discuss potentially contentions issues, power up your position by having supportive people there with you. For example, experts from your engineering, sales, and programming divisions. It's a psychological truth: An outflanked adversary may be so overwhelmed that he'll make on-the-spot concessions.

Defensive tip: If the other person shows up with a team of pinstripe commandos, grab one other person from your camp for emotional support. Two can take on 10, providing they have the necessary facts and knowledge.

Tactic #11: Fait accompli

Act as if a point has been agreed on, a concession given, or an issue decided, even though no such understanding has been reached. By acting as if a matter is a fait accompli, it becomes a fait accompli. Your implied message: "Leave me alone. I'm done!"

Go ahead—sign the papers. Just cross out what you don't like. Add what you want. Sign as indicated, and return the agreement. Heads up: Too many changes won't work. You're then transitioning from a fait accompli move to a potentially fatal "renegotiating the understanding move."

Defensive tip: Don't accept the other person's terms just because he's acting as if it were a "done deal."

Tactic #12: Call in the Missing Man.

As soon as you walk into the car dealership you spot a shiny black coupe that makes your heart flutter. After almost an hour of negotiating, your salesperson, Mr. Nice Guy, tells you, "It looks like we may have a deal." It's been a trying experience. You're glad its over.

As a formality, Mr. Nice Guy excuses himself to get management approval. He tells you to worry not. "It's just routine." When he returns, he sheepishly tells you "We have a glitch." News that's accompanied by a "frankly, I'm surprised" explanation.

Because of the big discount you were quoted for the shiny coupe, the manager said he had to *adjust* your trade-in allowance down by $550. "Your old model uses too much gas and doesn't sell all that well on our used car lot."

It's too late. Mr. Nice Guy has masterfully played out a "gotcha." Being emotionally committed, you're reluctantly willing to concede to the "price adjustment" and pay $550 more.

It's part of the language of the "Gotcha People." A price adjustment, rather than a price increase, conveys a false sense of "we're only correcting a mistake." To say "there is a problem" would make us feel uptight. But "glitches" are only potholes along the road to success.

The culprit? Higher authority: the *missing man.* Sometimes the *missing man* is nothing more than an illusion. Mr. Nice Guy may have been in the backroom sipping coffee with other salespeople supposedly seeking management approval.

Defensive tip: When you reach an agreement that is subject to approval by someone else's management, partner, spouse, department head, committee, board, or whatever, you may be negotiating against yourself.

To seal the other person's limited-authority escape hatch shut, ask at the very outset, "Do you have full authority?" If not, who does? Do you have authority over price? Terms? Delivery? If he does, then you're dealing with the right person.

Tactic #13: It's our policy.

"Sorry, I can't. It's our strict policy." That's the simplest argument you can make. After all, *policy* is a word that creates an aura of legitimacy by implying "The die is cast and please don't bother me with your requests."

Create policies on an as-you-need-them basis. The other person won't know whether they're freshly minted, or well-established, or consistently applied.

Tactic #14: Do an about-face.

Here's what I recently told a young lawyer:

> "We agreed to accept a $120,000 settlement. You never men-tioned terms. When you don't talk terms, that means lump-sum cash. Later we agreed that your client would instead pay $20,000 a month for six months with 10 percent interest on the unpaid balance.

> "Now you want payment to be spread over a year and no interest. I'm no longer willing to accept any payment over time. It's cash now or no deal."

You probably know how our negotiations ended. The other lawyer, who probably told his client about how well the negotiations were going, needed to save face. He was desperate to go back to the six-monthly payments with interest.

Usually, you keep bargaining to get something better than what you already have. My about-face maneuver was causing the six-month concession to disappear altogether.

Reversing course and taking concessions back is an unexpected move that will throw the other guy off stride every time.

Tactic #15: Turbocharge.

Recall how you raced through an argument because you had to be somewhere else for an important meeting. One that you couldn't be late for. In your anxiety to "finish up," did you make concessions that you wouldn't have otherwise made?

Deadlines create a sense of immediacy. A sense of immediacy creates pressure. Pressure causes action to be taken. Often, that action will be in the form of concessions given to meet the deadline.

Deadlines can be *personal* or *external.*

You're using a personal deadline when you say, "I'm flying off to my mountain retreat the day after tomorrow. I'll then be out of touch for two weeks. I'd have to drive 15 miles of unpaved mountain road to get an e-mail or fax." Okay, you may not have a mountain retreat, but you get the idea: You'll be out of touch. So it's now or never if the conflict is to be resolved.

When you say you must finish discussions by year-end for tax purposes, you're tying your cutoff date to an external deadline set by the IRS.

The closer and more specific the deadline, the greater the motivation for the other person to take action: "Negotiations must be complete by Friday at noon or there is no deal."

Tactic #16: Make an evaporating offer.

I was negotiating for a client. Their settlement demand was $75,000. Our offer was $65,000, which our client felt was fair. When our $65,000 offer was refused, we made an evaporating offer: $65,000 if the offer was accepted within five days. Thereafter, our offer would automatically decrease by $1,000 per day.

Time was marching on. The other side's opportunity to settle for $65,000 would soon be evaporating on a daily basis.

Sure, they could give the $65,000 offer all the thought and consideration they wanted. But their indecisiveness had a price. They had to ask themselves: Would more be accomplished by continuing to negotiate than would be lost as the settlement offer started to evaporate?

Tactic #17: Drag your feet.

Orchestrate a deadlock....

Does the other person have interests that can be crippled by a standstill? If so, don't make any moves. Let the deal appear to collapse. Because any deal is better than no deal at all, the other person will negotiate against herself.

Is the other person anxious? Lightly brake and you'll discover why he seems to be in a rush. Is there a desperate need? A hidden deadline? Another deal pending that is dependent upon an agreement being made with you first? Slowing things down will reveal the relative balance of power.

Light braking is calculated stalling....

"Alex, I would like to continue our negotiations but I just won't be available for the next few days."

By slowing, but not stopping the momentum, Alex's frustrations may well be translated into concessions.

As discussions get closer to a handshake, play on Alex's eagerness to finish up the negotiations. All of a sudden, the signed agreement that Alex thought was just a breath away is really somewhere up the street.

A foot-dragging finale can follow up light braking....

"By the way, Alex, I forgot to mention that...." "Oh, Sam one small thing that needs to be dealt with...." "Of course, Melinda, I expect to have a draft agreement by... ."

Tactic #18: The Uncertainty Effect.

"IS THAT A REAL CLOWN, OR SOMEBODY DRESSED LIKE ONE?"
—A YOUNG BOY ASKING HIS FATHER

Caltech conducted a simple experiment. Players bet on whether the next card drawn from a deck of 20 cards would be red or black. They were told how many of each color were in the deck. The players quickly calculated the probability of the next card being certain color. The risks could be calculated. The players comfortably assumed the risks they were taking.

In the second part of the experiment, the players were told how many cards were in the deck but not the number of each color. The players became hesitant. Less willing to gamble. This is known as the *uncertainty effect*. The *Wall Street Journal* notes that "the mere whiff of uncertainty can dramatically skew our decision-making."[4] An uncertainty example: The U.S. federal tax Form 2106 EZ had this "helpful" instruction: "An expense does not have to be required to be considered necessary."

Uncertainty causes people to be less inclined to take risks. Behavioral reality: Risk-takers are more likely to assert a position rather than trying to finesse a position. By creating uncertainty, there is less chance that your adversary will make heavy-handed assertions that may lead to his face-saving deal meltdown.

Tactic #19: Create scarcity.

"There is an element of appealing to scarcity that always works in every human being," reports the *Los Angeles Times.* That's why Frito-Lay offers "cheesy enchilada" Cheetos with the words "limited time only!"

printed on the bag. Why McDonalds in America offers a McRib sandwich as a promotional menu item just a few weeks at a time. Why the Gap sells limited edition jeans.

Create real or artificial scarcity. A cruise ship line told me that for their Greek Islands sailing, balcony cabins were almost sold out. If I wanted assurance of a balcony cabin, I should make an immediate deposit. When we boarded, we discovered there were quite a few balcony cabins that hadn't been booked. Those cabins were being assigned to other passengers as a complimentary upgrade.

Tactic #20: Threaten away.

A threat is knockout punch, a last-resort tactic that should first be cast as a warning: "If you can't deliver by Thursday at noon, then I'll have no choice but to cancel our order."

Only make a threat if the threat is well-thought-out and if you're truly prepared to carry it out.

And in the Looking Ridiculous Department: Never use a big threat to further of a small gain. A well-thought-out threat is relative to its purpose and objective.

A threat can't appear to be off-the-wall. "If you're not willing to refund my money, I'll have my lawyer sue you. The emotional distress you're causing me is going to cost you thousands." It has to be a natural and logical extension of your demonstrated anger, thwarted expectations, or your previously displayed attitude.

And it can't appear to be "over the top." Telling your girlfriend "I don't care if I ever see you again if you vote for the Democratic Party candidate" may not be what you really mean. Unless of course you're a dyed-in-the-wool Republican.

Chapter Summary

People are chronically human. When they're thrown off balance, they'll grant concessions to extricate themselves from an uncomfortable situation. In granting those concessions, they'll be guided by their emotions rather than by their sense of reason.

The fact that a Heavy Metal Move produces anxiety, tension, discomfort, stress, or pressure doesn't mean that it's an unconscionable tactic. Some moves just aren't as pretty as others.

Mediation, Arbitration, and Collaborative Dispute Resolution

Because the difference between justice and being right is called "legal fees"

"How much are we talking about?" The answer is always the same: It's your adversary who largely determines the cost of litigation. Litigation is about spending your time, money, and energy defending and countering what the other guy is throwing at you. If he's vindictive, he can turn litigation into a very expensive war of attrition.

Don't be fooled by the "let's go to trial" television dramas. They don't show the motions. The posturing. The look on your lawyer's face when she discovers that, until a few weeks ago, the judge assigned to your case against a contractor was a family law judge. You guessed right. The judge isn't that familiar with construction defect litigation.

In the New Normal, those in the know are opting for alternative dispute resolution, "ADR": mediation, arbitration, collaborative law, and their emerging conflict-busting hybrids.

Mediation

Waging peace

What is mediation?

Mediation is a process. An impartial person, the mediator, skillfully helps parties resolve conflict when they're unwilling or unable to resolve the conflict themselves.

What is a mediator?

☐ A mediator isn't a judge, an arbitrator, or a decision-maker. A mediator is a settlement facilitator. A skilled neutral.

☐ A mediator is a confidant, an empathizer, a harsh realist, a diplomat, and a magician.

☐ A mediator is an evaluator, a questioner, a reality checker, a persuader, and a peacemaker.

☐ A mediator is tenacious. He'll be persistent even when the parties have given up hope of resolution.

By the way, you don't need to be a lawyer to be a great mediator. Mediators can be child psychologists, contractors, architects, physicians, landscapers, and anyone with subject-matter expertise and a knack for problem-solving. Does that sound like you? Read on. You'll discover tips and tactics for being at the top of your mediation game—whether you're a mediator, a party, or a party's lawyer.

Why mediation?

Direct negotiations between the parties would be counterproductive because one of the parties has a no-holds-barred adversarial style.

Unlike court litigation, nothing happens in mediation unless *you* choose for it to happen.

Mediation is the litigation alternative. Here's the trouble with litigation:

With litigation, there is always the possibility of a runaway jury's extreme award or an appeal by the losing party. Mediation avoids outcome uncertainty. Here's how I caution clients that anything can happen with a jury. In Monte Carlo, Monaco, Charlie Chaplin entered a Charlie Chaplin Look-Alike Contest. He placed third. No one can ever argue that Chaplin's position wasn't strong enough for a slam-dunk win.

Wasting time is a natural part of the litigation process. Time frames are largely set by the court and your adversary. In mediation, dates, times, and places require your consent.

No one is comfortable in a courtroom. Court trials are public. Mediation is private.

A jury may be influenced on how a party speaks or looks, or that person's ethnicity. There are no appointed judges or juries in mediation. In mediation, the parties select the mediator who will provide biographical information and references.

Litigation takes an emotional toll on individuals, families, and businesses. Talk to someone who's in litigation and ask what he or she thinks about at 3:00 a.m.

It's hard to collect money from someone who thinks the judge or jury didn't understand the case.

There is a higher degree of commitment to a mediated outcome because the parties have *agreed* to do something rather than being *ordered* by a judge to do something.

Litigation always creates a loser and a winner. Litigation is about who's right and who's wrong. Mediation is about discovering creative trade-offs. In mediation, the parties settle and walk away shaking hands. In arbitration or litigation, no one will ever say, "This is the right outcome for both of us," and then shake hands.

In mediation, resolution is possible in stages, increments, or phases. Complex issues are effectively dealt with because the parties set and prioritize the mediation agenda.

Knowledge is power. You'll be better ready for trial if the mediation doesn't succeed.

Skilled mediators settle 80 percent or more of their cases!

The Mediator's Role

A mediator is a thermostat, not a thermometer

☐ **Conflict Assessor:** Assesses where the parties agree and disagree. Learns why the dispute wasn't settled directly by the parties. Was it because of a lack of communication? Emotions clouding good business judgment? Holding back information for "shock value" at time of trial? Not identifying issues? Information missing to evaluate the case? A desire to be retaliatory? Or were they swept up by the process into an uncontrollable web?

☐ **Communication Facilitator:** Keeps parties on track and the dialogue flowing by making transitional statements. Continuously summarizes, restates, questions, prompts reactions, and makes observations. Does not permit interruptions, arguments, disruptions, or cross-examination.

☐ **Transformer:** Puts a business or personal relationship back on track by focusing on the "people problems." Calls upon the transformative power of apologies, shares blame, flushes out misunderstandings, and acknowledges mistakes.

☐ **Coach:** Provides insight and perspective in private caucus meetings. Determines reasonable parameters. Points out flaws and unrealistic expectations.

☐ **Alternative Generator:** Generates fresh theories, options, and alternatives to keep the dialogue flowing and to better understand each side's interests and perceptions.

☐ **Resource Expander:** Suggests outside resources (such as engineers, technical personnel) to assist in clarifying and gathering critical information.

☐ **Reality Tester:** Tests the merits of a party's arguments in private caucus meetings.

☐ **Perspective Creator:** Asks, "If you can't settle and go to a court, how many depositions will need to be taken? How many days of trial preparation will be needed to show you're right? What is the cost of winning? How much more work/money/time will be needed if there is an appeal?"

❑ **Scapegoat:** Helps a party save face when his announced position needs to be changed. The mediator, as a scapegoat, takes responsibility for the needed change.

❑ **Process Controller:** Keeps power balanced so that the weaker party isn't overpowered by an aggressive, overbearing, or more skillful opponent. Never bolsters one side's case in the presence of the other side.

In a real-life mediated dispute between two partners, Joe and Jim, the testimony of the contractor who had done work for their partnership was critical. Joe claimed that in exchange for getting the job, the contractor inflated his construction costs and gave secret kick-backs to Jim.

Joe knew that the contractor was a devoutly religious man. He also believed that contractor would lie even if the mediator had him swear to tell the truth. Mediator's solution: The mediator would take the sworn testimony of the contractor at the contractor's church in the presence of the contractor's priest.

A mediator has a duty to be neutral and fair. But what should be done when there are under-represented or poorly represented parties? Impaired or incompetent parties? Parties who don't understand their rights? These are a mediator's ethical issues.

❑ **Scribe:** Keeps a record of offers, counteroffers, and agreed-upon settlement components. Upon reaching settlement, assists the parties in preparing a settlement agreement.

3 Pre-Mediation Tips

❑ **Tip 1:** Timing is critical. Don't rush into mediation without knowing the weaknesses and strengths of your case. An under-prepared case will be seen as by your adversary as a weak case.

❑ **Tip 2:** Parties need to reach a certain level of tension before they're amenable to mediation.

❑ **Tip 3:** Make a solid "in the ballpark" pre-mediation settlement demand. Popular myth: Without that demand you have more room to maneuver. Surprise demands usually result in no settlement.

Step 1: Convening

"Eighty percent of success is showing up."—Groucho Marx

Convening is a mediation term of art. Convening starts the mediation process and takes place to establish the procedural ground rules; define issues to be mediated; designate persons who will be participating (insurance adjusters, corporate officers), experts who will express opinions; agree upon mediation dates and places where the mediation will be held.

Joint convening meeting—now is the time to:

Discuss the mediator's fee. How much? Are there minimums? How are fees paid? What expenses and costs (travel, photocopying) will there be? Are there cancellation charges? Where will the mediation be held? Will either side present evidence? If so, what will the evidence be? Will witnesses or experts be testifying?

Agree in writing that all discussions are confidential unless otherwise agreed.

Decide who will attend. Will the folks in attendance have the absolute authority to make binding decisions? Can the president of a condominium homeowner's association make decisions without the board's concurrence? An insured party without the consent of her insurance adjuster? A corporate officer without Board of Director Authorization?

Identify where the parties agree and disagree. Will there be pre-mediation depositions? Pre-mediation on-site visits to relevant places? Pre-mediation briefs? What exhibits (such as contracts or e-mails) will be attached to your brief? Will briefs be for the mediator's eyes only? Or will they be exchanged with the other side?

Tip: Confidential pre-mediation briefs help the mediator quickly loop into the case. The brief doesn't need to be a formal document. Include information about the parties' historical relationship and the settlement efforts to date.

Private convening meeting—now is the time to:

Reveal sensitive information to the mediator in confidence. "Margaret" privately disclosed that "how much" was not as important to her as "how soon". She had terminal cancer and before dying wanted to set up an education fund for her grandchildren.

Meeting separately with the parties enables the mediator to determine how to best lessen hostility, avoid undue posturing, and set a platform for creative problem solving.

Step 2: Opening Joint Session
Dissident Land is now formally open

The parties are usually not present at convening if they have lawyers, but everybody is present at the joint session.

Comfortable people are less resistant, and more open to alternatives. Mediation is about emotion management, not emotion avoidance. In her opening statement, with all parties present, the mediator:

☐ Humanizes that process: "Sounds like we're in a terrible place right now. How do we get to a better place?"

☐ Thanks the parties for coming together in the spirit of resolution. She'll explain mediation and the role she'll play.

☐ Reminds the parties that "You're not negotiating with me, but with each other. I'm just helping."

☐ Encourages full participation. "Your attorney did a great job explaining your position. But is there anything you would like to add?"

☐ Identifies what's already agreed to and the remaining issues to be mediated. The mediator's credibility comes from showing she understands the situation.

☐ Announces ground rules, time frames, and constraints that were established in convening.

☐ Sets the agenda: Which issues are dealt with first? Which issues can be linked?

Tip: Hearing your opponent's statement is your chance to reevaluate and reassess your own position's strengths and weaknesses. And it's a chance to assess your adversary's jury appeal in the event there is no settlement.

The mediator may decide not to have a joint session (or have a joint session without opening statements) if she feels there is a great deal of personal hostility. On the other hand, an opening statement gives the parties an opportunity to vent.

Venting in a joint session can be a vital part of the resolution process. The ability to express feelings, frustrations, and emotions makes it possible to transition from anger and hostility to rational and deliberated conversation. No one will listen until they are ready to hear. Letting the parties "have their say" gives them the feeling that they "had their day in court."

The mediator also asks questions. But questions asked in joint sessions can't be pointed questions or questions that suggest the mediator's feelings about the case's merits and shortfalls. General questions that don't sound judgmental can be asked. "Can you tell us more about your reasoning?"

Step 3: Caucusing

A time for flexibility and innovation

The joint session is followed by the mediator's caucus meetings. These are private and confidential meetings held with one side at a time.

It's the mediator's judgment call as to who he shall meet with first. Should it be the party who didn't speak first at the opening joint meeting? The defendant or responding party? (Tip: The responding party may acknowledge valid portions of the claimant's case. Fewer contentious issues make the mediator's job easier.) The party that has the furthest to move for the conflict to be resolved? Or the party that seems dissatisfied with the opening joint session?

Head's up: Clients sometimes ask: "Why is the mediator taking so much time talking with them?" Mediation may take on an adversarial tone as the parties set up in "camps" for caucuses. It's an aura that gives rise to an "us" against "them" uneasiness.

For some, playing hardball seems a safe mediation strategy. After all, in the wings is a mediator standing at the ready to finesse a moderate ground for settlement. In caucus, the mediator discourages overreaching or counterproductive offers. Offers that are made as *final* offers, *best* offers, or *take-it-or-leave-it* offers.

A skilled mediator won't let the mediation turn into a contest of wills. Mediation is about settling, not winning. The caucus goal is to develop a realistic proposal that the mediator can then submit to the other side.

A mediator continues to shuttle between caucus rooms until a mutually acceptable path to resolution has been developed. Sometimes, there will be joint meetings between caucuses.

In caucus, a mediator unlocks sealed lips and closed minds by asking questions. When you ask better questions, you'll get better answers. In Chapter 8 and Chapter 10 you learned how to craft better questions.

Step 4: Finessing a Resolution

The mediator has a choice of three paths: distributive, integrative, and evaluative. Most mediators segue between paths.

Distributive mediation: What one side gains, the other side loses

Distributive bargaining is a tug-of-war. A contest of wills over a "fixed pie." No future relationship with the other side is at stake. It's what's called a "Zero-Sum" Game.

The mediator's job is to keep the negotiations going by maintaining an atmosphere for realistic, reasoned, give-and-take.

The "Mediator's Dance" is a behavioral reality: Each concession made will likely be half of that party's prior dollar increase or decrease. For example, if your first offer is $1,000, your next offer will likely be $500 more ($1,500), and then $250 more ($1,750).

The dance's reality continues: Each concession a party makes will likely take twice as long as the one before it. Settlement will likely be a number reached halfway between the parties' first two reasonable offers. The mediator's goal is to get a reasonable offer from each side. It's only then that the mediator can suggest splitting the difference.

A real mediated distributive case

Here's a case I use in my workshops. What would you do if you represented one of the parties? If you were the mediator?

Greg is an adult with a child's intelligence. Greg has been steadily employed for 10 years as an animal shelter assistant. He had an excellent credit rating, charging the necessities of life and timely paying his car payments, rent, and other ongoing obligations.

Knowing Greg loved animals, he was approached by Gary, a con-artist, offering a horse stable investment opportunity. Greg would be a part owner and would be in charge of caring for the horses.

Greg fell for the scam, giving Gary his personal credit information and permission to use that information to help finance the stable project.

Gary used that information to help Greg open four American Express credit card accounts. Gary was a supplemental cardholder on each account. Gary's address was used as the billing address. Greg had no prior American Express accounts.

Gary used the accounts he opened in Greg's name for his own personal purposes and kept the credit ball in the air by making periodic payments to American Express. When the ball fell, Gary had racked up $40,000 in charges.

American Express collectors started to call Greg, who, feeling intimidated, paid American Express $1,000 over several months.

American Express sued Greg for $40,000 arguing that (1) Greg's identity wasn't stolen. Greg intended for the accounts to be opened and gave Gary the personal information necessary to help him open the accounts. (2) American Express had no way of knowing that Greg believed that the charges would be used for a horse stable venture. (3) American Express had no way of knowing that Greg had a child's intelligence. (4) Greg made payments on the accounts.

Greg's lawyers argued that it should have been apparent to American Express that something wasn't right. They further alleged that American Express "ruined Greg's credit."

Pre-trial mediation was ordered by the Los Angeles County Superior Court. I was the court appointed mediator. Mediation ended with American Express feeling its legal position was justified. Nonetheless, wanting to do "the right thing," it dismissed its suit. If American Express hadn't made an "emotional decision," what would you as a mediator have done?

Integrative mediation: Increasing the size of the pie

An integrative approach is to expand the pie so both parties can "win," It's sometimes called win-win mediation. How do you expand the pie? By not having a tug-of-war. Instead, focus on developing mutual gain options. I call these options "pie expanders."

Put on your creative hat. Develop options. Brainstorm. Be inventive. Tailor options to make them fit. If they don't fit, scrap them and try new options. A waste of time? No. Unworkable options reveal impediments to settlement. Unworkable options keep the dialogue going.

Consider these pie-expander trade-offs. The magic word is *if*. "I'll concede doing _____ *if you're willing to*_____.

❐ **Finance:** Cash or credit. Interest rates, terms, discounts for early payment. Quantity discounts. Prices of extras and add-ons. Collateral or security.

❐ **Risks:** Warranties. Guarantees. Repair obligations.

❐ **Delivery:** When, where, and how will deliveries be made? Who pays the carrier? Who is responsible for damage? Late penalties. Packaging.

❐ **Relationship:** Exclusive selling rights. Advertising allowances. Sole supplier rights. Guaranteed minimum purchases. Training. Ongoing support. Duration of contract.

❐ **Specifications:** Allowable variations. Quality tolerances.

Evaluative mediation: Summoning "the Agent of Reality"

Some mediators have a more "facilitative style" and seek "win-win" results. Others an "evaluative style." In private caucus, they evaluate and disclose their opinion as to whether a party's arguments are meritorious. Wearing an evaluative hat, the mediation takes on an adjudicative tone as the mediator becomes *The Agent of Reality* focusing on the legal issues. Causation. Experts' opinions. Damages. Predicting trial outcomes. Quantifying potential damages. Estimating going-forward trial costs. Discussing the likelihood of expensive appeals.

Evaluative mediation is only effective if it is credible. An evaluative mediator needs to be someone whose judgment the parties respect. Subject matter expertise is important. For example, in a workplace dispute, a labor lawyer may be the best horse for the course. **Tip:** The later evaluative statements are made, the more effective they'll be.

Doing what it takes to get the dispute settled, skilled mediators deftly blend facilitative and evaluative styles.

STEP 5: Closing

It's not over until it's over

A mediator should never quit when there is an agreement in principle. Agreements should be in writing *before* the mediation concludes. Critical terms to be included in the mediated agreement include: Specific actions that need to be taken. By whom and when. Penalties for not taking timely action. Procedures for resolving issues that may come up. Dispute resolution procedures for alleged violations.

Arbitration

Truce or friction?

Binding arbitration is an adversarial process. A private trial. Unlike court litigation, arbitration usually takes place in an office setting. Unless the parties agree, arbitration doesn't require adherence to strict, court-mandated, procedural rules.

The arbitrator is an impartial person chosen and hired by the parties. A written arbitration agreement empowers him to make binding decisions just as if he were a judge in a court trial. In fact, many arbitrators are retired judges. The arbitration agreement defines the arbitration's scope: Who will be witnesses? Which experts will testify and for whom?

The right of appeal from binding arbitration is very limited. If the arbitration award doesn't need to be court-enforced, then by agreement of the parties, the arbitration proceedings are confidential.

Arbitration Hybrids

- ❐ **Final offer arbitration (sometimes called "baseball arbitration"):** Each side agrees to settle for a predetermined amount. The arbitrator, after hearing the case, chooses which of those two amounts will be his award.

- ❐ **"Night baseball" arbitration:** Each party sets its demand amount. The amounts aren't revealed to the other party or to the arbitrator, who holds them in a sealed envelope. The demand amount that is closest to the arbitrator's award will be the binding arbitration award.

❑ **High-low arbitration:** Before the arbitration, the parties jointly set award high and low amounts. It is agreed that the arbitrator's only job is to determine liability. If the defendant is found liable, the predetermined high amount will be paid to the plaintiff. If no liability is found, the defendant shall pay the predetermined lesser amount to the plaintiff.

❑ **Incentive arbitration:** The parties elect to have non-binding arbitration. However, they have a binding agreement setting the amount of a penalty that will be imposed if a party rejects the arbitrator's non-binding monetary award and takes the case to court trial. If the rejecting party's position is not improved in trial, the penalty is imposed.

❑ **Bracketed arbitration:** Limits risk by the parties jointly placing upper and lower limits on the arbitrator's award discretion.

❑ **Neutral expert:** Retained jointly by the parties, the expert gives his opinion on limited factual or legal issues. The parties agree in advance whether that opinion will be binding or just advisory. For example, the expert may determine motor vehicle accident fault by analyzing skid marks, ascertaining collision damage, measuring braking distances, and determining speeds. Those findings may be binding on the parties, or just advisory to the arbitrator who may agree or disagree with the expert's conclusions as to was at fault. If binding, then the arbitrator has to abide by the expert's conclusions. The arbitrator can still make awards on related issues such as the compensation for an injured party's pain and suffering.

Mediation/Arbitration Hybrids

There are several *variations* of or *combinations* of mediation and arbitration:

❑ **Separate Med-Arb:** If mediation has *failed*, the mediator changes hats and becomes an arbitrator who makes a binding decision on all unresolved issues. The mediator's power to change hats encourages the parties to reach their own settlement on impasse issues.

❐ **Integrated Med-Arb:** As the mediation *progresses*, the mediator becomes an arbitrator, making binding decisions on stalemated issues. This "on an as-needed basis" ability makes it possible for the mediation to continue on issues that aren't stalemated.

❐ **Opt-Out Med-Arb:** Parties agree that if resolution isn't reached in mediation, an arbitrator, *but not the person who was the mediator*, takes over and makes binding arbitration awards. **Tip:** Consider having the potential opt-in neutral attend the mediation joint sessions so she'll be prepared to arbitrate.

❐ **Final Offer Med-Arb:** Following an unsuccessful mediation, the mediator, now acting as an arbitrator, makes a binding award decision by selecting one of the party's final mediation offer. The mediator/arbitrator must choose one of the two competing offers, but nothing in between. To avoid this risk, the parties will make a reasonable final offer in mediation.

Tip: If there are multi-issues (single party with many issues) or multi-party (single issue with many parties) disputes, consider mediating part of the dispute while using other approaches for the balance of issues.

❐ **Arb-Med:** The arbitrator acts as a mediator only after first having heard the case in arbitration. The arbitrator reveals his binding decision only if there was no agreement in mediation.

Collaborative Law

Because an ex-spouse is forever

Some folks think that agreeing to mediation is a sign of weakness, a sign that one is prepared to make even more concessions and compromises.

Some folks believe that in private caucus meetings, an adversary will lie and unfairly influence the mediator.

Some folks believe that a mediator will play mind games to lower their reasonable settlement expectations.

The collaborative way is free of a mediator's arm-twisting. Free of an arbitrator's focus on absolute rights and wrongs. Free of lawyers saying what clients expect to hear from their hired guns. Free of behind-closed-doors caucus meetings. Free of disagreeing and battling experts. Free of a party holding back the disclosure of critical data and information.

To best assure a level playing field, a written participation agreement obligates the parties to be fair, reasonable, and respectful to each other and to the collaborative process.

The parties hire attorneys (collaborative attorneys) to assist them throughout the process. Collaborative attorneys sign a disqualification clause in the participation agreement. That clause prevents them from going to court if the collaborative case doesn't settle.

A collaborative coach, who is often a licensed mental health professional, is sometimes hired in emotionally charged cases to coach one or both parties. It's the collaborative coach's task to keep emotions and retaliatory behavior in check.

A collaborative team includes jointly sponsored retained experts such as appraisers, tax experts, and accountants. Their task is to openly provide impartial advice and opinions.

If circumstances warrant, a case manager functions as a facilitator. Unlike a mediator, the case manager can't caucus or be evaluative. Their task is to preserve the collaborative process aura by prioritizing issues, keeping discussion balanced and flowing, and strategically calling upon the skills of the impartial retained experts.

Collaborative sessions take place in a meeting room. An underwhelming place where adversaries don't pitch their case to a "for-hire stranger"—a mediator or arbitrator.

A place where there is a *feeling of safety* because a collaborative attorney can't threaten litigation, having signed a disqualification clause.

When collaborative is the chosen alternative, it sends a positive message: *Let's resolve our issues side-by-side in the spirit of good faith, fair dealing, openness, and transparency.*

Collaborative seeks change—change in the way the other party sees things. More importantly, change in how they feel. How the other person feels flows from how you are. Not from how things are. You're always both: The messenger and the message. In mediation, the mediator is the messenger. In collaborative, you're the messenger—front and center.

The energy that drives home settlements is a hard to swallow. Participation Agreement's Disqualification Clause: If there is no settlement, your lawyer is contractually obligated to disengage and not take the case to trial. Ouch!

Collaborative attorneys risk losing long-term, or potentially long-term, clients to another lawyer. The New Normal's super competitive market makes that possibility a sleep-wrenching reality. Not so gutsy if you're a divorce lawyer. Unless your client is a serial spouse, the client relationship is usually over when it's over except for the ritual of exchanging holiday greeting cards.

Clients also have good reason to be concerned about changing horses midstream. After all there's home team rapport in place. Feelings of confidence and comfort made possible by a client's investment of time, money, and energy.

Changing attorneys means starting anew, looping a new player into an expensive and time-consuming learning curve. And if that isn't enough to be concerned about, there's the possibility that a wily opponent will purposely block settlement for no reason other than to cause a highly capable adversary to bow out.

Is potential disqualification of your lawyer worth the risk? The collaborative way is a different way of managing conflict. It emphasizes the restructuring of relationships. It works by collectively considering each person's needs—openly and completely. Sharing information. And most importantly building an aura that better keeps relationships cordial, if not intact.

If MediCollab (mediation/collaborative) is provided in the participation agreement (or later agreed upon), the case manager changes hats and mediates the impasse issue. Or, at the request of the parties, an impartial mediator is hired to help resolve any issues still in contention.

Chapter Summary

ADR is about *you* having choices.

You have the choice to participate or not participate in one of the ADR processes. *You* have the choice of who will serve as mediator, arbitrator, or case manager. *You* have the choice to set outcome parameters (for example, in arbitration high-low limits, binding or nonbinding outcome). *You* have the choice of cost control limitations (for example, the number of witnesses or depositions).

Unlike court litigation, nothing happens unless *you* choose for it to happen.

Cross-Cultural Persuasion

Because the world gets smaller every day

"When in Rome, do as the Romans do." Not "When in Rome do as the Romanians do."

In our global economy, there's a good chance you'll be buying or selling a product or service from someone you never met. Someone who works for a company that you've never visited.

When negotiating a deal or settling a dispute, instead of racing to the airport, you'll probably seek resolution by telephoning, e-mailing, or electronically conferencing. Whether you're sitting at a keyboard or at a negotiating table, the basics are the same. And the task is the same: to influence a desired outcome.

Sorry, there's no "one size fits all" approach. No, it's not enough that you have a warm smile. Not enough that everyone says "you have a great way with people."

I'm a lawyer in Los Angeles. With globalization, my client base has changed dramatically through the years. I now represent folks from every corner of the globe. Some of those folks live a world away. Others live just down the street. But you don't leave cultural notions about trust, relationships, morality, and ethics behind. In ways big and small, those notions define who and what we are.

Cultural sensitivity isn't about trying to be like the other person. You can't be who you're not. Nor is it about trying to make the other person more like you.

There's a difference between "deep culture" and customs.

Customs are about protocol. What you need to know to be polite—who expects a kiss on both cheeks, who expects you to bow, and who expects a gift.

Deep culture is about the other guy's values. Values that make him who he is. Just as your values make you who you are. Values are non-negotiable. They can't be changed any more than you can change hearts and minds. When you understand a person's values, you understand their tendencies. Tendencies because no one is ever exactly how they are supposed to be.

This chapter then is about cultural tendencies—theirs and yours. And about how to reconcile the differences. Changing your expectations. Changing how you deal with, and relate to, the other person.

Early in my law practice I had a rude cultural awakening. I was hired by a group of prominent Middle Eastern businessmen. Flush with oil money, they had come to the United States to invest in real estate.

They would personally identify properties and negotiate the deal. My job was to follow the parade, making sure everything ran smoothly to conclusion.

The first property was a nursery about 2 miles outside of Phoenix, Arizona. Nurseries sit on large parcels of land. The plants and trees they sell occupy a lot of room.

John and Marie were selling because they wanted to move closer to their grandchildren in Michigan.

My clients' plan was to operate the nursery business for a few years. When Phoenix urban sprawl stretched out to the nursery, they would then shut down the nursery business and build apartments.

The price was a little more than a million dollars cash. At signing, a $50,000 check was deposited in a neutral bank with instructions to pay the deposit to John and Marie upon the transfer of ownership. Title to the business and land would transfer in 60 days. The $50,000 deposit would be the full penalty payment if my clients cancelled.

As soon as the contract was signed, John started preparing for his move north: He quickly found a buyer for his Arizona home, and signed a contract to buy a Michigan house that he and Marie both liked. They enrolled their daughter in a private Michigan school. By the time 55 of the 60 days had lapsed, John was packed. The movers were at the ready. Friends were tearfully hosting goodbye potluck dinners.

Then I got "the call." "Tell John he can keep the $50,000. The price is way too high. We'll still buy if the price is reduced to $920,000."

John was beyond angered. He was also trapped. His life had been changed in ways that would be expensive and almost impossible to unwind. He and Marie had little choice but to agree.

A few months later, I learned that the price reduction tactic was pre-planned. And yes, if John said "no reduction," my clients still would have closed at the million-dollar price. Even without a reduction, they considered the price a "real bargain."

John and Marie learned the hard way that in some cultures, a deal is a deal when hands are shaken. In others, a deal is a deal when contracts are signed. In still others, a deal is only a deal when the check clears the bank.

Were my clients immoral and unethical? In the eyes of someone raised in the United States they might be. However, in their eyes, it was "business as usual."

What would my clients have done if they had found John's wallet with $1,000 tucked inside? No question. The wallet and money would have been quickly returned to John. In my client's culture, exploitive business moves are accepted. And that's what this chapter is all about: cultural tendencies.

Will Time Be Used as a Tool or as a Resource?

It's not the same old one-on-one anymore

Will decisions be made quickly? Or will decisions come only after time is spent in "getting-to-know-you" meetings? Will you need to invest time socializing before getting down to serious business?

There are cultural differences as to what time is about and what it means.

Monochronic cultures: Your appointment time is 3:00 p.m.

GREAT MOMENTS IN SCIENCE: EINSTEIN DISCOVERS THAT TIME IS ACTUALLY MONEY. – A GARY LARSON CARTOON CAPTION

For me, time is about punctuality, my willingness to wait, and how long I'm willing to listen to long-winded explanations. Time is a critical dynamic of my lifestyle, as it is for most Americans.

Time is compartmentalized and managed. We save time, buy time, spend time, waste time, and make time. We take time commitments seriously. Classes start and end on time. Work schedules have beginning and ending times. Appointments are on time. Yes, an exception is waiting in a doctor's office in the company of outdated magazines.

Monochronic cultures include the American, German, Canadian, and Northern and Western European countries.

Polychronic cultures: Your appointment time is "sometime in the afternoon."

Being late for an appointment or taking time to get down to business is the norm. Time is flexible. Creating and strengthening relationships is more important than time ticking away. Plans are changed easily and often. It's expected. Don't be surprised if you wait all day for a meeting, only to be told to come back tomorrow.

Polychronic cultures include Latin American, Mediterranean, Arabian, Philippine, Indian, African.

Heads up: Some cultures use delays to show a loss of interest or kill a deal. The Chinese use delays hoping you'll show your negotiating hand first or grant concessions to keep things on track.

Tip: Don't reveal travel plans to return home. Instead, offer to spend as much time as it takes to resolve any misunderstandings. Here's a classic deadline ploy that was sprung on me:

I was in Costa Rica negotiating for some American businessmen who were considering building a local distillery that would convert cane into alcohol. On the night of my arrival, I was invited to a party at the home of the cane grower with whom I would be negotiating. In seemingly idle conversation, he asked how long I would be in San Jose. I told him I would be leaving in three days.

It seemed that only I wanted to talk about cane availability, price, and terms. It was thrust and parry. No sooner would I initiate a business conversation than he would change the subject.

After two and a half sun-drenched days filled with coffee plantations, the Mercado Central, country club lunches, and city tours, he finally initiated the discussions that I had been anxiously waiting to pursue. He knew my deadline. I did not know his. He also knew that I had other commitments back in Los Angeles, that I would feel pressure to make concessions in order to take home a deal, and that clients don't like flying their lawyer to Costa Rica only to have him come back empty-handed.

Is Their Style Linear or Circular?

Monochronic cultures deal with one subject, or part of a subject, at a time in a linear style that values orderliness.

Polychronic cultures deftly deal with segments or topics all at the same time. Closure isn't needed in one area before jumping onto the next. Like plate spinners, the pieces are juggled with ease. Discussing matter #1, jumping to matter #2, jumping to matter #3, and then jumping back to matter #1. It's a "circular style" that values agility.

When meeting with my French restaurateur client, Philippe, he would simultaneously answer phone calls, speak with a never-ending procession of vendors and staff. Hold mini-meetings in English and French, and, yes, talk business with me. Yet throughout it all, Philippe was fully in charge. When I told a group of lawyers about Philippe, one got us all laughing by asking "Doesn't Philippe know the reason God invented time is so you don't have to do everything at once?" It was my favorite comment of the day.

At the end of a two-day workshop, I asked my Dubai workshop class if the way I presented materials, answered questions, and shared information would have been different had the class been taught by an Arab. Did they find my linear logic and sequential style too restrictive and too confining? Did it make learning easier? Their answer confirmed what I already knew: It's easier for a circular style to adapt to a linear style than it is for a linear style to adapt to a circular style.

How Do They Make Decisions?

Collectivism and *individualism* refer to the connection people have to their work and society. Are they working to accomplish something for themselves? Or are they working for the greater good of their country, their family, or their company?

Collectivist cultures see work as a way of life rather than a means to a better life.

Right is what's right for the team. Negotiating power flows from team consensus. Decisions aren't unilaterally made. Calls to the home office should be expected.

On March 11, 2011, a historic 9.0-magnitude undersea earthquake struck off the Japanese coast. Its mega thrust created an extremely destructive, 23-foot tsunami wave that caused the partial meltdown of three nuclear reactors. Japan calls them the "Faceless 50"—the Fukushima nuclear plant workers who stayed on the job keeping the reactors from melting down. According to Mark Magnier, in a March 17, 2011 article for the *Los Angeles Times*, their "collective consciousness is almost second nature....The group-first mentality is nurtured by years of conditioning from parents and teachers.... Some even contend it is a sensitivity bred into the Japanese soul. There is pride in the apparent lack of looting, egregious price gouging, and the orderly acceptance of the need to ration water and gasoline."

In China, a team's collective decisions may have been made well in advance of your meeting. When you do meet, their predetermined collective decision is announced.

Collectivist cultures include Asian and Latin American.

Individualist cultures view work relationships as less meaningful than personal relationships and the quality of life. Accomplishing tasks, not team relationships, is job #1. Power is vested in individuals. Independent thinking and self-determination are valued, and people speak for themselves.

Individualist cultures include American, Dutch, French, British, and Nordic.

Marketers are aware of cultural differences. According to Hana Albers in a May 11, 2009 article in *Forbes*, Samsung had differing ad campaign pitches for the same phone: For the individualist American market, the advertising message was "I march to the beat of my own drum." For the collectivist Korean market, the campaign focus was on how the phone would keep families connected.

Who Makes the Decisions?

High-power distance cultures respect authority, status, and rank differences. Differences that may be based on age, sex, seniority, competency, schooling, and sometimes connections. The company's more powerful individuals initiate and end conversations. Dictate who interrupts. Who is interrupted. Speak as often and as long as they want. Make undisputed decisions. The boss is always right because he's the boss.

Bypassing a superior can kill any chance of conflict resolution.

High-power distance cultures include Latin American, South Asian, and some Arab cultures.

Low-power distance cultures believe in equality and strive for equal power among people. Group members consult with each other. The boss is only right when he gets it right.

Low-power Distance cultures include American, Israeli, Nordic, Swiss, Australian, and German.

Are They Uncertainty-Adverse or Uncertainty-Tolerant?

Uncertainty avoidance is about risk-taking, whether one feels comfortable with uncertainty, unpredictability, and ambiguity, and whether the decision-maker is more likely to belabor every point or make "shoot-from-the-hip" calls.

Cultures less likely to take risks: The decision-making process is more methodical. Slower. Detail-oriented. Comfort comes from relying on formal rules, procedures, and standards.

High-risk-avoidance cultures include Greek, Italian, Spanish, Mexican, French, Portuguese, Guatemalan, and Japanese.

Cultures comfortable with risk: They require less information, and have fewer people involved in the decision-making process. Decisions are made on a "gut" level. What feels right. Working through a business hierarchy is seen as inefficient. There's a strong individual achievement motivation. A motivation that prompts a willingness to take risks.

Sam was from the Middle East. Sam heard that a new car dealership facing hard economic times was anxious to sell. Sam had cash and was anxious to buy. Without the assistance of lawyers or advisors, Sam bought the dealership over a dinner meeting. The deal was memorialized in a handwriting that was less than two pages long. If the printing had been smaller, one page would have been enough.

The sale was not disclosed to the car manufacturer (one of the "Big Three") until a few weeks after possession of the dealership had changed hands. The manufacturer declined to honor the sale—Sam had no new car dealership experience.

My client Joe ended his four days at a Las Vegas hotel owing the casino about $600,000 in gambling debt. Joe had been given credit and kept signing markers as his run of bad luck continued. He asked me to negotiate a discount by arguing that it was unfair and unreasonable for the casino to continue extending credit to someone who had been drinking (but wasn't drunk) and was clearly obsessed with trying to win. A small discount and an interest-free payout program were negotiated.

After the case was settled, the casino manager visited with me. "Bob, the big risk-takers are the folks you'll see in our special high-stakes gaming rooms. For the most part they are Asians and Middle Easterners. When it comes to risk, they have nerves of steel. It's those risk-takers that we cater to."

Are You Ready to Hear What They Don't Say?

Context is probably the most critical dynamic in the art of influencing outcomes. It's also the hardest to define.

Context is best defined with examples:

Having the best argument or the most charisma is not as important as showing you care about the relationship being forged in high-context cultures. At a rug dealer in Morocco, the owner wouldn't talk about his selection of rugs without my wife and me first sitting and visiting over tea.

Treating contracts as binding documents can be insulting and detrimental to a high-context culture relationship. But being too informal can be detrimental in a low-context culture.

Americans view negotiating as a process of offers and counteroffers. Japanese view negotiating as a process of information-sharing.

In Arab cultures, negotiating is aggressive and is part of the process of developing a personal relationship. But Japanese and Chinese view negotiating as dysfunctional. Instead they use indirect rather than confrontational approaches.

In the United States, we embrace our right of personal freedom, and the dignity and entitlement of ordinary persons. The experience of individualism and the rule of law. That's our context. It's what give us a clear sense of who we are and where we're going. My culture forecasts my tendencies and how I relate to others.

High-context cultures attribute little value to words alone. Much is left to what isn't said. Culture explains what isn't said. For words to have value, their express meaning has to be coupled with their unstated, implicit meaning. Implicit meaning is imparted by the surrounding context—cultural history, the role of relationships, customs, and shared beliefs.

A commonality of knowledge, sense of purpose, and views among members are assumed. Knowing how to act in a situation, what's "right," is acquired through experience and custom. Through context.

Remember: We're talking about tendencies. Context is not high or low in any absolute sense. Each action and reaction falls somewhere along a high-to-low continuum. A 55-year-old Japanese businessman may view things differently than his 25-year-old son. But in some ways, and at some times, the father and son are at different points on the same high-context continuum.

High-context cultures include Chinese, Italian, Greek, Japanese, Korean, Arab, Mexican, and Spanish.

Tip: If you're using an interpreter, ask for your interpreter's impression of what isn't being said, but is implied.

Low-context cultures lay out everything in words. Little is assumed. The express message means everything. What's important is what is actually said. What is written. Verbal and nonverbal communications are wordier. Lacking implicit information, there's a need to convey more factual information. Every word is meaningful.

Low-context cultures include Canadian, German, Nordic, and French.

Heads up: Interactions between high- and low-context peoples can be problematic. For example, Japanese do not distinguish between personal and business relationships. High-context Japanese may find low-context Americans to be offensively blunt. Americans may find Japanese secretive, devious, and not forthcoming with information.

Bridging Differences: Who Gives In?

Americans are appreciative of compromise as a solution to impasse. For the French, compromise is sometimes seen as an insult to carefully crafted logic.

In the Middle East, compromise may give rise to a negative sense of giving in. My Israeli clients see things in black and white. Right and wrong. Fair and unfair. They are slow to compromise.

My Egyptian client, Ali, compromises only after he exhaustingly considers and evaluates each and all of his alternatives. He isn't concerned with expediency, but with what's his best-deliberated alternative.

Some cultures don't treat compromise as the answer to impasses because of a need to maintain self-esteem.

Here's the reality: Each side wants the discussions to go well. Cultural sensitivity is understanding and talking about the differences in how you and they act and feel. It's too easy to get annoyed with people who don't think the way you do. Sympathize with their views and patiently work towards resolution.

Do you compromise? The answer is a simple one. How badly do you want to do the deal?

19 Tips From the Persuasion Pros

☐ **Tip #1:** Just because someone speaks English doesn't mean he shares your values. It's possibly still his second language. If English is his second language:

- Speak slowly. Keep it simple. Use short, common words that don't have more than one meaning.

- Don't use slang expressions, idioms, or figures of speech: "A ballpark number is...." "Let's put that on the back burner." "I don't want to play hardball." "This is what's eating me." "Run that past me again." "Think outside the box."

- Don't use industry jargon, corporate-ese, legal-ese: "Here's the loophole." "Tipping point."

☐ **Tip #2:** Use visual aids to avoid information overload. Color-coding charts and graphs show how individual areas are connected.

☐ **Tip #3:** Be aware of their possible influences: their economy political influences, corporate culture and corporate restraints, and individual personalities. (The other guy may just be a "difficult" person. Every culture has them.)

☐ **Tip #4:** Strategize an agenda with the other side. Should primary or secondary issues be discussed first?

□ **Tip #5:** Think win-win. Having a global mindset is not about outgunning, outfoxing, and out-maneuvering the other side. It's about trust and positive feelings.

□ **Tip #6:** If the other side becomes manipulative, unethical, or deceptive, don't retaliate. Stop the negotiations and say why you find his behavior unacceptable.

Common unacceptable tactics: misleading about one's authority, or lack of authority, to make a deal. Demanding last-minute concessions to avoid the deal being killed.

□ **Tip #7:** Be protocol- and customs-sensitive. Learn what's expected with regard to the use of first names. What to wear. Conduct at social events. The importance of business cards. After-hours socializing. Gifts: how, when, and what. Body language and personal space: how close and how far? Americans feel a firm handshake is a sign of sincerity and honesty. In the Middle East, a gentle grip is appropriate. Arab men may not shake hands with a woman.

□ **Tip #8:** Be professional. Don't be too informal. Don't over-personalize. Don't place blame. Relationship-building is about trust, dependability, and candor. Being too nice or too kind can make the person-to-person linkage suspect.

□ **Tip #9:** Be polite. Japanese are hesitant to do business with people who are seemingly impolite or brash.

□ **Tip #10:** Who are you? Let others know your experience and accomplishments without being full-of-yourself. Send advance information about you and your company. In Asian countries, it's important that your counterparts know your status.

□ **Tip #11:** If there is a misunderstanding, slow things down. Try to figure how the problem arose and work to remedy it. Discuss cultural differences. Collectively plan how to best proceed. Seek general agreements rather than specific agreements.

□ **Tip #12:** If you are using an interpreter, speak to your counterpart, not to the interpreter. Yours or theirs. Have your interpreter make sure that the other side's interpreter is accurately reporting what you're saying.

□ **Tip #13:** Learn as much as you can about each member of the other side's team. Be aware of status considerations:

Who should sit next to whom? Who should talk first? To whom will you address your comments?

❑ **Tip #14:** Plan in advance how you will deal with impasses. There is no one right way. Understand their culture and the importance of self-esteem and saving face.

❑ **Tip #15:** Understand their culture's common negotiating tactics and plan how you will neutralize or counter them.

❑ **Tip #16:** Having a winning global mindset requires listening more carefully than you are accustomed to. Well-thought-out questioning. Preparation that is up to the task at hand. The versatility to change approaches until you find one that accomplishes your goal.

❑ **Tip #17:** We all feel emotions. But in some cultures, expressing those emotions is considered immature. Displaying anger can be destructive in Asia because it disturbs the harmony necessary for relationship-building. In Asia, it's generally best to keep your feelings to yourself.

❑ **Tip #18:** Leave your wheeler-dealer, roll-up-your-shirt-sleeves, go-for-goal style at home. Most often, it will be counterproductive. The key to winning is focusing on interests and needs, not positions. What are their needs? What are their concerns and problems?

❑ **Tip #19:** Remember the 11th commandment: "Thou shall be cool."

Chapter Summary

Spend less time learning to use chopsticks or how to speak their language (an interpreter will do a better job anyway) and more time sensitizing yourself to the other person's deep-rooted cultural tendencies. From that understanding flows the power of versatility. The power to influence outcomes. The power of a global mindset.

Epilogue
Because now you're ready to win any argument!

"IF YOU HAVEN'T FOUGHT WITH EACH OTHER, YOU DO NOT KNOW EACH OTHER."
—CHINESE PROVERB

No matter who you are, what you do, whatever the situation, there are bound to be arguments.

Arguing. There's the rough and tumble of the norm, the amateur's game. And then there's the pro's game of winning arguments by knowing how to make, manage, and move an argument. Knowing what to say, how to say it, and when to say it.

On our journey, you've discovered that self-mastery separates the amateurs from the pros. How you walk the valleys and how you maneuver the turns. Whether you're able to get out of your own way. An empowering sense of self-command and a constant state of assessment is only possible when you possess a *still center*.

You've discovered that a Consent Zone is a no-blows environment. An underwhelming aura that sets the tone, mood, and cadence of the argument to follow. It's a virtual place where you'll finesse rather than force. A place where others will be less resistant to you and your ideas.

You've discovered how to bring an in-your-face attack to a screeching halt, and how to defuse hostility, anger, and aggression.

You've discovered that ideas presented intellectually won't persuade others emotionally. That it's never enough that your argument *sounds right* (logical), it must also *feel right* (emotional). Feeling right is about how *you are* rather than how *things are*. The way to win is to blend approaches:

Likeability. *Hi-touch*: the approaches you need to get others to feel what you feel. Believe what you believe. See what you see.

Logical. *Analytical*: the approaches you need to get others to think what you think. Understand what you understand.

You've discovered that you can't win an argument with someone who feels they're being talked into something. *Surgical strike questions*, rather than allegations and assertions, win arguments as the other person discovers for himself or herself why it makes sense to do it your way.

You've discovered that the right words will zoom your argument from ho-hum dull to compelling, that just the right word is itself a powerful argument.

You've discovered that you can prompt your desired response by tapping into, triggering, and stimulating highly predictable emotional needs that can be satisfied by your desired for outcome. Planned action = desired reaction.

You've discovered that when your argument is in a letter or memo, the other person can reread, absorb, and understand—luxuries that a listener doesn't have. But presenting you argument in writing doesn't provide in-person feedback, so you cannot be sure whether you've broken through. In every instance, strategize your alternatives. If writing your argument is the way to go, you've learned how to make your writing convincing and compelling to the max.

You've discovered that there is a difference between what's *efficient* and what's effective. An e-mail or telephone call may not be the best way to advance your argument, but you now know how to be at the top of your telephone game.

You've discovered an argument-winning platform for achieving long-terms results and preserving family, friends, and coworker relationships that you just can't walk away from.

You've discovered that the tactics you'll use when arguing to a group are different than those you would use when it's one-on-one.

You've discovered that, in the New Normal, winning depends on being able to call upon, and to defend against, Heavy Metal Moves.

You've discovered that cross-cultural negotiation, persuasion, and conflict resolution requires a global mindset. Having a "nice way about you" isn't going to cut it. It may even make things worse.

And a final note as our journey ends: Just as conflict is an inescapable part of the human condition, so too is deception. Our deceptions are tolerated when they aren't destructive and when they help reach a result that is not exploitive.

Each of us is a self-contained business. That is truer today than ever before. There is no such thing as a permanent job or real job security. You are what people say about you and what people think about you. That's your personal following. That's your portable goodwill.

Now go out there and win arguments!

Notes

Chapter 1

1. Johnson, Greg. "Gambling Ads: Group Wants Help Lines in Gambling Ads." The Los Angeles Times, June 19, 1998. Page D-1.

Chapter 2

1. Nicholas, Peter and Carla Hall. "The Recall Campaign: Schwartzenegger Tells Backers He "Behaved Badly." The Los Angeles Times, October 3, 2003. Page 1.

Chapter 4

1. Braun, Stephen. "Cattlemen Want Oprah to Eat Her Words." The Los Angeles Times, January 21, 1998. page A-1.

Chapter 7

1. Pund, Daniel. "Maybach 57-Road Test." *Car and Driver Magazine.* August. 2003.

Chapter 9

1. Newman, Barry. *Wall Street Journal*, May 13, 1997.

Chapter 12

1. Posner, Howard. "Once More With Sarcasm." *California Lawyer*. Nov 2010.

Chapter 16

1. Berman, Lee Jay. "It's Time For Heavy Metal Mediation!" *Mediation Tools.com*

2. Burley, Ron. "Sometimes You Need to Be a Bully to Get What You Deserve. *AARP* Magazine March/April 2007.

3. Gellene, Denise. "Pricer Pills Are Seen As Better." The *Los Angeles Times*, March 5, 2008.

4. Lehrer, Jonah. "How Uncertaintly Cripples Us." The *Wall Street Journal*, January 8, 2011.

Index

About the Author

Larry King, former host of *Larry King Live*, says that "Bob Mayer is a lawyer's lawyer." Bob received both his business and law degrees from the University of California at Berkeley. A veteran been-there, done-that lawyer, Robert Mayer and his firm represent clients big (foreign governments, including Venezuela, for whom the first heavy-weight prize fight ever held in South America was negotiated) and small, famous (some of America's best-known actors and athletes) and infamous, negotiating deals on everything from amphitheater developments to the sale of zero vintage aircraft.

In addition to being a professional mediator and practicing law, Mayer conducts "How to Be a Mediator" and "Negotiating Tips, Tricks, and Tactics" seminars and workshops that have been presented for MBA. and law students and for various private businesses, trade groups, and professional associations.

Mayer has interviewed more than 200 of the world's masters—the legendary street and bazaar merchants of Bombay, Istanbul, Cairo, and Shanghai—gathering bargaining, haggling, and horse-trading tips for travelers headed for marketplaces around the world. When he can get away, he is a popular cruise ship lecturer who shares those secrets in light-hearted talks to cruise ship passengers bound for destinations where a marketplace mentality is a must to be a top-seeded shopper.

For more information, visit Bob Mayer's Website, *www.TheWay-ToWin.net.*

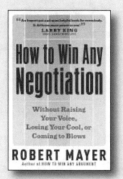
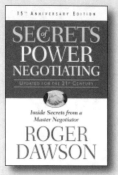

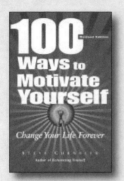
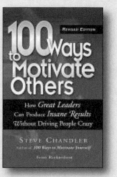

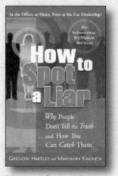